DONALD W. TREADGOLD STUDIES
ON
RUSSIA, EAST EUROPE, AND CENTRAL ASIA

Books in the Treadgold Studies series honor the memory
and distinguished contributions of Donald W. Treadgold,
who taught Russian history at the
University of Washington from 1949 to 1993.

Perils of Pankratova:
Some Stories from the Annals of Soviet Historiography
Reginald E. Zelnik

Reggie Zelnik reading to his grandson, Jaxon Zelnik Stuhr,
at Reggie and Elaine's home, December 2003.

PERILS OF PANKRATOVA
Some Stories from the Annals of Soviet Historiography

Reginald E. Zelnik

Contributions by
Laura Engelstein
David A. Hollinger
Benjamin Nathans
Yuri Slezkine
Glennys Young

Published by the Herbert J. Ellison Center for Russian,
East European, and Central Asian Studies, University of Washington

Distributed by the University of Washington Press
Seattle and London

Printed in the United States of America
12 11 10 09 08 07 06 05   5 4 3 2 1

Russian, East European, and Central Asian Studies Center (REECAS)
Henry M. Jackson School of International Studies, University of Washington
www.depts.washington.edu/reecas
Previously published Treadgold Papers are available through REECAS.

University of Washington Press
P.O. Box 50096, Seattle, WA 98145
www.washington.edu/uwpress

Library of Congress Cataloging-in-Publication Data
Perils of Pankratova : some stories from the annals of Soviet
historiography / Reginald E. Zelnik ; contributions by Laura Engelstein,
David A. Hollinger, Benjamin Nathans, Yuri Slezkine, Glennys Young.--1st ed.
p. cm. -- (Donald W. Treadgold studies on Russia, East Europe, and
Central Asia)
Includes bibliographical references.
ISBN 0-295-98520-8 (pbk. : alk. paper)
1. Pankratova, A. M. (Anna Mikhailovna), 1897-1957. 2.
Historiography--Soviet Union. 3. Marxian historiography--Soviet Union. I.
Zelnik, Reginald E. II. Series.
DK38.7.P28P47   2005
907'.2'02--dc22   2005001329

The paper used in this publication is acid-free and 90 percent recycled from at least 50 percent post-consumer waste. It meets the minimum requirements of American National Standard for Information Sciences—Permanence of Paper for Printed Library Materials, ANSI Z39.48-1984.

CONTENTS

ABOUT THE CONTRIBUTORS

Laura Engelstein is Henry S. McNeil Professor of History at Yale University. She is the author of *Moscow, 1905: Working-Class Organization and Political Conflict* (Stanford University Press, 1982), *The Keys to Happiness: Sex and the Search for Modernity in Fin-de-Siècle Russia* (Cornell University Press, 1992), and *Castration and the Heavenly Kingdom: A Russian Folktale* (Cornell University Press, 1999).

David A. Hollinger is History Department Chair and Preston Hotchkis Professor of History at the University of California, Berkeley. His recent writings have appeared in *Aleph, American Historical Review, The Cambridge History of Science, Church History, Constellations, Daedalus, Diacritics, Harper's*, the *Jewish Quarterly Review*, and *Philosophical Studies*.

Benjamin Nathans teaches modern Russian and modern Jewish history at the University of Pennsylvania. His book, *Beyond the Pale: The Jewish Encounter with Late Imperial Russia* (University of California Press), appeared in 2002.

Yuri Slezkine is Professor of History and Director of the Institute of Slavic, East European and Eurasian Studies at the University of California, Berkeley. His most recent publication is *The Jewish Century* (Princeton University Press, 2004).

Glennys Young, editor of the Donald W. Treadgold Studies on Russia, East Europe, and Central Asia, teaches Russian and European history, as well as peasant politics, at the University of Washington. She is the author of *Power and the Sacred in Revolutionary Russia: Religious Activists in the Village* (Pennsylvania State University Press, 1997).

DONALD W. TREADGOLD STUDIES ON RUSSIA, EAST EUROPE, AND CENTRAL ASIA: AN INAUGURAL VOLUME

THIS IS THE INAUGURAL VOLUME IN A NEW SERIES, *Donald W. Treadgold Studies on Russia, East Europe, and Central Asia.* One of the most distinguished historians of Russia of his generation, Donald W. Treadgold taught history and international studies at the University of Washington from 1949 to 1993. During that time he trained many Russian historians. He also wrote seven books, including *Twentieth Century Russia*, of which there have been eight editions. Among the most significant of his many contributions to the profession, both on the national and international level, were his two terms of service as editor of *Slavic Review*, the journal of the American Association for the Advancement of Slavic Studies (AAASS). The AAASS also honored him with two of its awards, for Distinguished Contributions to Slavic Studies, and for Distinguished Service.

The publication originating this series, *The Donald W. Treadgold Papers in Russian, East European, and Central Asian Studies*, was created on the initiative of Professor Daniel Clarke Waugh when Professor Treadgold retired from the University of Washington in 1993. When Professor Treadgold died in 1994, it became a memorial series in honor of his profound, and lasting, contributions to the University and to the profession. The first editor of the series was Professor Sabrina Ramet, whose hard work and vision helped to make the series a lasting one. I became the editor in 2001 when Professor Ramet moved to another institution.

Many individuals have helped make possible this inaugural volume, which is the first to be published under joint agreement with the University of Washington Press. The arrangement was worked out over many months by Pat Soden, Director of the University of Washington Press; Michael Duckworth, Executive Editor, University of Washington Press; Professor Stephen Hanson, Director, the Herbert J. Ellison Center for Russian, East European, and Central Asian Studies at the University of Washington; and myself. The financial support of Mrs. Alva Treadgold and the Treadgold family have been essential to the success of the Papers and now to its new embodiment in these *Studies*.

Glennys Young
Editor
Donald W. Treadgold Studies on Russia, East Europe, and Central Asia

ACKNOWLEDGMENTS

Glennys Young

AS EDITOR OF THE DONALD W. TREADGOLD STUDIES on Russia, East Europe, and Central Asia, I would like to express my thanks to those who have aided in the publication of this Memorial Volume for Reggie Zelnik. Special thanks are due first to Reggie's wife, Elaine, his daughter, Pam, and his son-in-law, Mark Stuhr, for their help in providing the photographs and in supplying the information that appears in some of the captions, and to Reggie's brother, Martin, for his helpful advice. It has also been a pleasure to work with the other contributors: Laura Engelstein, David A. Hollinger, Benjamin Nathans, and Yuri Slezkine. I am grateful to Eve Levin for invaluable counsel, always freely given, at many points in the publication process. This volume would not have been possible without the enthusiastic support and essential efforts of Professor Stephen Hanson, Director of the Herbert J. Ellison Center for Russian, East European, and Central Asian Studies, and Marta Mikkelsen, the center's Associate Director. Ted Cotrotsos's talents as a designer have greatly enhanced the volume, and have provided an authoritative template for this inaugural issue of Treadgold Studies. Sigrid Asmus copyedited the text for the volume with exquisite attention to detail and much-appreciated good cheer. John Mason expertly proofread the volume. I am also grateful to Martha Walsh and Michael Biggins for answering proofreading queries. Finally, thanks are due Michael Duckworth, Executive Editor at the University of Washington Press, for his thoughtful and creative suggestions regarding the production process, and to everyone at the press for welcoming this project and helping it reach a wider audience.

PREFACE

Glennys Young

REGGIE ZELNIK'S DEATH ON MAY 17, 2004, has robbed us of a remarkable scholar, mentor, campus leader, and citizen. At the Memorial Service held on August 29, 2004, on the Berkeley campus that he selflessly served for four decades, one speaker found the words that were on everyone's minds: Reggie was "academia at its human best." Indeed, Reggie epitomized the finest that academia has to offer, but he did so in a way that was "impenitent" and "unclichéd," to draw upon words that Reggie himself liked to use.[1] His unique qualities as a person and a scholar make it wonderfully impossible, as Bill Rosenberg put it, to "memorialize" him "appropriately."[2]

Since Reggie can't be appropriately memorialized, this is something of an unmemorial volume.[3] It does not aim to capture or fix in one place all that Reggie was, contributed, and stood for. Rather, it modestly seeks to join the many individual and collective efforts that his family, friends, colleagues, and students have made in bearing witness to what, with Reggie's death, we have lost. Its modesty bears emphasis. Although to many, Reggie was larger than life (all the more for being effortlessly so), he was a humble person. He would not want to be made larger than life. Had he heard himself praised as "academia at its human best," he would have gently reminded us to keep the emphasis on "human" rather than the superlative. Had he been notified in advance of a memorial volume, one imagines that he would have responded much as he did when he was presented with the festschrift edited by Jerry Surh and Bob Weinberg upon the occasion of his sixtieth birthday: he was touched, yet stunned, to be so honored.[4] One imagines that he might have accepted a memorial volume only on the condition that it would help to advance the field of Russian history, historical inquiry, and citizenship. This is what the present volume seeks to do.

The origins of what was to be a very different volume go back to early 2003, when, as Editor of the Donald W. Treadgold Papers in Russian, East European, and Central Asian Studies, I invited Reggie to be the 2004 Donald W. Treadgold Memorial Lecturer, an invitation that meant that the Treadgold Papers would publish the manuscript on which the talk was based. Reggie graciously agreed, even though he noted that because he had recently completed the volume on the Free Speech Movement that he edited with Robert Cohen,[5] and had been making "subsequent bookstore appearances," he was not sure what he would present. In July 2003 he wrote that he would "give my UW talk on the historian Anna Pankratova—her life and travails as the leading labor historian of the Soviet Union from the 1920s to her death in 1957."[6] On April 19, 2004, he gave the Treadgold Memorial Lecture, "Perils of Pankratova: Some Stories from the Annals of Soviet Historiography." He had given a similar presentation, based on a precirculated paper of the same title, at Stanford University on February 26, 2004. Shortly before he visited the University of Washington, he sent me the last version of what he called his "little mini-monograph" on Pankratova, which he had earlier promised to do, so as to "expedite the editorial/publishing process and get it out a little sooner." It is this nearly finished version that his colleague in Russian history at Berkeley, Yuri Slezkine, has prepared for publication, complemented by translations of excerpts from transcripts mentioned in the text, and introduced in relationship to Reggie's classic books and articles.

Reggie's death changed not only the volume's purpose, but also its content and format. Consulting with Reggie's wife of forty-eight years, Elaine Zelnik, who was integral to everything he did, and with his family, the contributors felt it would be fitting to present Reggie's study of Pankratova at the center of a gathering of essays about Reggie's scholarship, teaching, university service, and citizenship. Focusing on Reggie's landmark publications in labor history, his work-in-progress, and the study on Pankratova, Laura Engelstein shows that all of Reggie's scholarship has "withstood shifts in scholarly fashion" (and will continue to do so) because of his "interest in personal experience behind collective movements, his rejection of easy explanatory schemes, and his persistent attachment to what remains a central question for Russian and Soviet history"— that is, how those working in factories came to think of themselves as part of a class. As Ben Nathans notes in his essay that evokes what it was like to be his student, Reggie's "greatest legacy at Berkeley and in the field of history lies in his role as teacher and mentor, understood in the broadest sense." In tribute to Reggie, the volume also includes an appendix that lists Reggie's doctoral students, along with their major publications. Many of these works grew from their dissertations; others, while on subjects different from their dissertations, nonetheless reflect Reggie's influence. Reggie also served, it should be noted, on numerous other doctoral committees in

Reggie Zelnik at the
Berkeley-Stanford Conference,
April 16, 2004.

Russian and European history at Berkeley, and gave his treasured counsel
to students elsewhere. Yet it was not only in training historians-in-the-
making, and giving riveting lectures (delivered without notes) to under-
graduates that Reggie served his institution and its students. As David
Hollinger observes in his essay, Reggie "gave and gave and gave" to Berkeley,
for over four decades, with his "reasoned criticism" as a leader on the
campus, not only in his irreproducible role in the Free Speech Movement
and in the campus antiwar movement but throughout his career, in less
well-known and sometimes more behind-the-scenes ways.

Like the historical subjects whose lives he so remarkably reconstructed, Reggie's own contributions cannot be captured by a "fixed
schema of classification."[7] Classifying an essay on Reggie as only about his
scholarship, or teaching, or service is necessarily artificial and limiting, as
the content outstrips the initial category. Reggie's efforts to "fathom the
inner complexity," as Laura puts it, of individual lives "behind collective
movements" call to mind the "person-centered" approach that, as Ben defines
it, was at the core of his teaching. Reggie not only transmitted that
approach in the questions he posed on page after page of works in progress,
but was "above all interested," as Yuri writes, as a "historian, teacher,
colleague, and friend . . . in human beings—their lives, their choices, the
stories they told about their lives and choices, and the stories that others

told about their lives and their stories." It is also artificial, as David's contribution suggests, to separate Reggie's roles "as an academic and his politics as a citizen." In both settings, Reggie's signature was "the same style of reasoned, evidence-based argumentation," always delivered with uncommon respect and grace. Although Reggie never used the classroom or his own scholarship to advance his own political views, he knew how to be "simultaneously political and professional while keeping the two in their own domain." Scholarship, teaching, and citizenship were, for Reggie, simply different contexts in which he impenitently insisted on the same moral principle—the dignity of the individual.

Nor can the centerpiece of the volume—Reggie's tour de force on Pankratova—itself be easily classified. As Reggie reconstructed Pankratova's stormy journey through simultaneously difficult political, historiographical, and moral seas, his companions, as Yuri writes, were the familiar "themes and subjects that preoccupied him throughout his life." Anna Pankratova was, like many of those who captured Reggie's historical imagination, a worker and a fighter, yet someone who was, in a title he considered for the piece, "neither devil nor angel." And yet, something new is also emerging here in Reggie's choice of this subject, broadly considered. Reggie's most memorable historical subjects—Semën Kanatchikov, Vasilii Gerasimov, Ernst Kolbe, to name but a few—were male. Yet his last and just as memorable subject was a woman whose struggles as an academic, as well as an ordinary Soviet citizen, Reggie reconstructs in all their complexity. During World War II Pankratova's life journey took her to Kazakhstan, in Soviet Central Asia, where her "personal experience" trumped Marxist internationalism in leading her, as Reggie puts it, to a "self-appointed position as guardian of the national rights of the Kazakhs."[8] This is not the first publication in which we find Reggie examining ethnic issues. In 1961, the MA thesis he wrote at Stanford was titled "The National Question in the Russian Social-Democratic Labor Party, 1898-1914." His *Law and Disorder on the Narova River: The Kreenholm Strike of 1872* (1995) "touches on," as he wrote, "the relations among the empire's various nationalities, mainly Estonians, Russians, and Germans, each holding differing positions in Russia's structure in this corner of the empire."[9] But this is the first time that Reggie examined issues of ethnicity and nationalism in the Soviet, and specifically Central Asian, context. Finally, this is the first publication in which Reggie, whose major contributions focused on labor history in Imperial Russia and who also wrote superb essays on the Civil War and Gorbachev eras, directly discusses the interwar years, World War II, the late Stalinist period, and its immediate aftermath. These works are listed in Reggie's last curriculum vitae, which is the second appendix to this volume. At a point in his career when prominent academics often prefer to stay on familiar ground, Reggie was developing and growing, a trait that Nicholas Riasanovsky, Reggie's colleague for over four decades at Berkeley, emphasized to me a few days before the Memorial Service.

We can only imagine, with great sadness, how Reggie would have kept developing and growing. He had already sketched the framework, as Laura discusses in more depth in her essay, of a book on the history of the strike in the period from 1789 to 1917 in Russia, France, and Germany. In Seattle, during the discussion that followed his Treadgold Memorial Lecture, he talked about the need, in the historiography of the Soviet period, for more "case histories," a genre, as Reggie noted in the introduction to his book on the strike at the Kreenholm factory, "in which a story is put together with attention to the larger but nonetheless specific historical context in which it occurs—its social geography, as it were—and to the various issues that it raises."[10] One can well imagine him writing other "case histories" for the Soviet period beyond that of Anna Pankratova. Yet, just as Reggie's legacy can be memorialized only imperfectly, we cannot predict what his future scholarly path may have been. Reggie would have surprised us. There can be no doubt, though, that wherever his agile mind would have taken him, his work would always exemplify what he believed was "essential to most historical writing": that it "capture and reflect the excitement, uncertainty, and improvised quality of the experience."[11] If his always developing scholarly agenda remains tragically incomplete, its dynamic unpredictability, together with his tremendous achievements, nonetheless sets a course for others to follow, each in their own way. We mourn Reggie's absence from our midst as a scholar, a teacher, and a citizen. And yet—to invoke the final words of Vartan Gregorian that closed the Memorial Service—his example remains with us, as we turn in our own directions. For these reasons, I like to think of this volume not as an end, but as a beginning.

NOTES

1. For "impenitent," see Reginald E. Zelnik, *Law and Disorder on the Narova River: The Kreenholm Strike of 1872* (Berkeley and Los Angeles: University of California Press, 1995), p. 6. He used "unclichéd" in less formal writing. For helpful comments on an earlier draft, I thank Laura Engelstein, David Hollinger, Eve Levin, Ben Nathans, and Yuri Slezkine.
2. This comment was made in an e-mail posting to the Allan K. Wildman Group for the Study of Russian Politics, Society, and Culture in the Revolutionary Era. Reggie, a good friend of the late Allan Wildman, was vital to the activities of this group.
3. I adapt here Ben Nathans's 1996 toast to Reggie as the "Undoktorvater."
4. Gerald D. Surh and Robert E. Weinberg, eds., *Russian History/Histoire Russie (Festschrift for Reginald E. Zelnik)*, Vol. 23, Nos. 1-4 (1996).
5. Robert Cohen and Reginald E. Zelnik, eds., *The Free Speech Movement: Reflections on Berkeley in the 1960s* (Berkeley and Los Angeles: University of California Press, 2002).
6. E-mail letter of July 31, 2003.
7. Zelnik, *Law and Disorder*, p. 1.
8. Yuri Slezkine, "Reggie's Bebels: An Introduction," p. 3 in this volume, and Reginald E. Zelnik, *Perils of Pankratova*, p. 36 in this volume.
9. Zelnik, *Law and Disorder*, p. 2.
10. Ibid., p. 1.
11. Ibid., p. 2.

PERILS OF PANKRATOVA
Some Stories from the Annals of Soviet Historiography

REGGIE'S BEBELS: AN INTRODUCTION

Yuri Slezkine

THE BIOGRAPHY OF ANNA PANKRATOVA was not meant to be the culmination of Reggie's work. In many ways, however, it is—not only because it proved to be the last thing he ever wrote, but also because it incorporates so many of the themes and subjects that preoccupied him throughout his life.[1]

Anna Pankratova was—like Reggie—a labor historian. She was his colleague, his scholarly predecessor, and his guide to archival sources. She was a permanent presence in his footnotes and thus, one imagines, in his memory. Her documentary collection on the history of the Russian labor movement was one of the most important books in Reggie's life. It was cited in the first article he ever published and it was on his desk the day he died.[2] Asked why he had decided to write about Pankratova, Reggie used to say that she interested him because she had worked on similar things under very different circumstances. Or rather, because she had worked on similar things in spite of her very different circumstances.

If we think about them carefully, the historiographical debates in which she engaged, ugly as they were because of the Stalinist ethos of denunciation and character assassination, and simplistic as they often were because of the ritualistic yet plastic discourses of "Marxism-Leninism" (whatever that really was as a "methodology"!), entailed issues that any serious historian would have to engage and that did not lend themselves to easy visions of right and wrong.

Anna Pankratova was—like most of Reggie's subjects—a worker. Or rather, she had grown up in a world that she herself would have described as proletarian.

She was a child of the working class if ever there was one. Her father, Mikhail Fedorovich, was a factory worker of peasant background, probably the son of serfs, who had left his Kaluga village to seek work in Odessa. Her mother, Elizaveta Nikiforovna, a peasant from Saratov

3

province, took in laundry and did other kinds of menial day labor to help keep the family afloat, especially after the death in 1906 of the father, who had been seriously wounded in combat in the Russo-Japanese War.

She went to work at a factory when she was fourteen years old, and remained committed to her roots—and the ideology that had made them glorious and intelligible—for the rest of her life. Her youthful struggles against "bourgeois professors" were as much about different social styles and past experiences as they were about ideology, and even late in life (as many photographs make plain) "Academician Pankratova" looked decidedly, and perhaps deliberately, proletarian compared to her bitter rival "Academician E. V. Tarle" and her close friend "Academician N. M. Druzhinin."

Or rather, Anna Pankratova was—like most of Reggie's subjects—a would-be worker, a former worker, an uncertain worker. Reggie was not particularly interested in what workers did at work; he was interested in how people became workers, stopped being workers, reacted to being classified as workers, and related to people who were not classified as workers. He was curious about "unique historical types who managed to combine" diverse features "in ways too intricate to be reduced to finite points on a linear graph of social change"; pointed repeatedly to "the difficulty of fitting the life of even a single individual (let alone whole segments of society) into the mold of a neatly delineated social typology"; and was endlessly fascinated by how people from different social locations talked to each other, depended on each other, and, occasionally, became each other.[3] On the one hand, "meeting Mitrofanov . . . filled Plekhanov with the mixed feeling of 'pity and awkwardness,' one that would not be unfamiliar to a student of race relations in America today." On the other, "had [Khalturin] continued his formal education, like a close childhood friend from his village who joined him in the capital but then took the path of higher education, we would be discussing Khalturin the 'student,' not the 'worker'."[4] And of course it was not always possible to tell the difference, anyway: in the "circles" of the 1870s, workers became students while students became teachers, and during Berkeley's Free Speech Movement (as Reggie wrote in 1966 in an article entitled "Prodigal Fathers and Existential Sons"), "the thesis is the students in the streets; the antithesis is the faculty attempting to keep the students off the streets; and the synthesis demanded is the faculty leading the students down the streets."[5] Whether the synthesis demanded was ever achieved is open to question; what remained constant was Reggie's interest in dialectical, or perhaps mythological, metamorphoses on the way to greater inner unity. Semën Kanatchikov was a peasant's son who became a worker, a "worker intellectual," a "professional revolutionary," a Party functionary, and finally a professional former worker and "Old Bolshevik." In his introduction to Kanatchikov's memoir, Reggie called his life story "a journey completed, a journey that, if not really circular, was ultimately a disguised return of the prodigal son."[6] When, nine years later, Reggie learned of Kanatchikov's final fate, he chose to end his essay about it on the same note of ironic circularity: "His crime, one that except for 'counter' before the word 'revolutionary,' must have had an ironically familiar ring to Kanatchikov, earned him a sentence of eight years in a work camp. He had served about four at the time of his death."[7]

Pankratova's final defeat was much less decisive than Kanatchikov's, but her life's journey, as Reggie describes it, consisted of the same principal stages and revolved (assuming it was circular) around a comparable set of traits, commitments, and "intellectual and moral certainties." Pankratova spent more time being an intellectual and administrator than did Kanatchikov or any other of Reggie's Bebels, but the quality she shared with them all, as well as with Reggie himself, was her willingness to fight for her "intellectual and moral certainties"—"within the political parameters [she was] faced with." Reggie was primarily interested in industrial workers, but some of the most memorable portraits he ever created are those of Kreenholm's manager, Ernst Kolbe, who was defeated by his own intransigence; Estland's governor, Prince Mikhail Shakhovskoi, who accomplished (and agonized) so much within the political parameters he was faced with; and of course their later—and, for Reggie, possibly earlier —incarnations: Berkeley's Chancellor Edward W. Strong (1961-65) and the University President, Clark Kerr (1958-67). Pankratova was a worker who became an administrator (and a historian); she was both a Gerasimov and a Shakhovskoi; she was, in a sense, halfway between Kanatchikov and his biographer. Reggie's story of Pankratova's life begins at the conclusion of Kanatchikov's autobiography and ends with her death in 1957, about a year after Reggie graduated from college.

Pankratova was—like most of Reggie's subjects—a fighter: not a spectacular or uncompromising one, but a fighter nonetheless, all the more interesting for being unheralded and inconsistent. As far as Reggie was concerned, the apparently unimportant was important because it revealed "the social and political tensions that were buried beneath the surface." The Kreenholm strike was not a part of "the canon of permanent historical reference points"; Gerasimov was "marginal" in every conceivable way; and Kanatchikov was "not a major figure in the political history of modern Russia, not even an important link in the chain of Russian revolutionary history." All of them, however, "give flesh and personality to otherwise colorless sociological categories" and make possible "the dramatic tension that is essential to most historical writing if it is to capture and reflect the excitement, uncertainty, and improvised quality of the experience of the actors." Reggie chose his subjects because they were ordinary and extraordinary, socially representative and unique. He preferred strikes to both daily routine and revolution, and he found "constrained dissidents" more interesting, and more congenial, than either prophets or conformists.[8]

Reggie's main subjects were people and events. He wrote—"impenitently," as he put it in his introduction to *Law and Disorder on the Narova River*—about things happening to people and about people making things happen. He told stories.

> The perspective of historians, of course, is not that of the actors, much as we must strive to reconstruct their points of view. As historians we must, in a sense, start afresh, reworking the partly conflicting stories told by participants, witnesses, and investigators . . . into a new narrative, one that evaluates and reevaluates their varying points of view by seeking out sources and perspectives of which the actors were deprived.[9]

The result is a new story: complex, crowded, and multilayered, but carefully (and impenitently) plotted to include an exposition, a climax, a denouement, and an epilogue. Eight out of nine chapters in Reggie's first book, *Labor and Society in Tsarist Russia*, are devoted to a richly textured description of the physical, social, political, legal, and intellectual world of St. Petersburg's industrial workers. It is only when we get to the last chapter that we realize that what we have been reading is in fact a magnificent introduction to the story of the Nevsky factory strike of 1870. In the short narrative of one dramatic conflict followed by a one-day trial, the book's central themes come together—and truly come alive.[10]

In *Law and Disorder on the Narova River*, the proportion of action to exposition is reversed, with various serial data and "broader structural conditions and constraints" woven "into a narrative tale, with the analysis of their significance (including their significance to the principal players) integrated whenever possible into the narrative itself." What attracted Reggie to the story of the Kreenholm strike was the "theatrical quality of the narratives to which it lends itself"—and, indeed, after the stage has been set, the cast introduced, and the curtain raised, we witness a drama in three acts held together by the unities of place, time (broadly conceived), and action; followed by an exhaustive resolution ("Outcome, Epilogue, Conclusion," including two "Endgames"); and "revisited" in a postscript that contains an eyewitness account within an autobiography within a biography within the larger story of the Kreenholm strike of 1872.[11]

The structure of Reggie's brilliant long essay on the history of law and disorder during the Free Speech Movement of 1964 is essentially the same: the dramatic tension is reinforced by the same three unities; each act of the drama is built around a theatrical public confrontation, and the epilogue revisits the main themes from a vantage point outside the plot (except that here the eyewitness and the historian are one and the same person, so that the autobiography is "integrated whenever possible into the narrative itself," making the whole work even more complex and more unified).[12] *Perils of Pankratova* is quite similar, even though it belongs to a different genre. The story follows the life of one individual, but it is organized around a series of cataclysmic events that test the protagonist's character, reveal the limits of the "structural conditions and constraints," and involve public scandals, limited casts, and provisional resolutions: "the Pankratova affair" (the First Betrayal); the "Pokrovskii affair" (the Second Betrayal); the "Bekmakhanov affair" (the First Battle); the "Korol'chuk affair" (the Second Battle); the "Burdzhalov affair" (the Last Battle).

But, of course, *Perils of Pankratova* is a biography, and its main unity is one of human life. Those of Reggie's books and articles that were not about particular events that pitted human beings against each other were about particular human beings and about events that informed and transformed their lives (thereby becoming "personal experiences"). As a historian, teacher, colleague, and friend, Reggie was above all interested in human beings—their lives, their choices, the stories they told about their lives and their choices, and the stories that others told about their lives and their stories. *Perils of Pankratova* is about both Pankratova's life and the perils of Stalinism. Its purpose, according to the author, "is not to make a definitive assessment of [Pankratova's] very complicated career, but to take us on a tour through the high points (or low points) of the muddy, messy world of Soviet historiography as exemplified by Pankratova's professional and political life." Its other purpose, also according to the author, is to make sense of the muddy, messy world of Soviet historiography in order to figure out how to "talk about Pankratova," "imagine" her "troubled yet in its own way creative life," and offer a "moral assessment" of the choices she made and did not make.

Reggie was interested in the way history was made by—and ultimately made up of—human beings. There would have been no recognizable Free Speech Movement in Berkeley "if Mario[Savio] hadn't existed," and there would have been no "August Revolution" of 1991 in Russia if Gorbachev had not encouraged so many Soviets "to be prepared for the day of reckoning."[13] But Reggie was equally interested in the way human beings were made by history (understood, in this case, as a succession of personal experiences). One of the stated objectives of the essay on the Free Speech Movement is to give the reader "a sense of the variety of attitudes present within the faculty, and of the shifting subjectivities that evolved over time as events outstripped the fixed positions of individuals and drove them to reassess their previous positions."[14] Similarly, according to Reggie, it is not so much Lenin's temperament, particular government policies, or the conspiratorial legacy of late populism that best explain the elitism of *What Is to Be Done?*; it is Lenin's experience with "Russia's real, living working class," including the peculiar group of worker *intelligenty* epitomized by Babushkin and Kanatchikov.[15] And it is not only Pankratova's Marxist internationalism that led "to her self-appointed position as guardian of the national rights of the Kazakhs"; it is also—emphatically—her "personal experience" of life among real, living Kazakhs.

Reggie's subjects are shaped by their experiences, but they are not fully defined by them. "Most people work within the political parameters they are faced with," but they are not reducible to those parameters or any other structural conditions and constraints. They are all free to make choices.

The choices they make are based on their sense of who they are. Fascinated as Reggie was by "the shifting subjectivities that evolve over time," he was not willing "to abandon the notion of a unified, time-bound personality altogether." His subjects are endowed with unique traits and are propelled—and burdened—by enduring convictions, commitments, and loyalties. "Was Pankratova," he asks, "really so lacking in principles that we cannot discern any consistency in her ideas and in her actions?" The answer is clearly no—in the case of Pankratova and in the case of all those Reggie found worthy of scrutiny (and companionship). When Kanatchikov received the news of his father's death, he felt terrible sadness but also some relief that the confining sense "of 'obligation' and 'responsibility'" he had always associated with his father would finally "vanish forever." Not quite true, Reggie argues: "the feeling of 'obligation' and 'responsibility' . . . would remain with Kanatchikov long beyond his father's death." After all, Kanatchikov's journey was also a "disguised return" home. And so, mutatis mutandis, was Gerasimov's (which Reggie described as the story of "abandoned and reclaimed foster child"). And so, in a sense, was Pankratova's (framed as it was by two battles: the one she fought "as a schoolgirl in Odessa" and the one that killed her a long lifetime later).[16]

Ultimately, however, the choices they made were based on their common moral sense. The physical, social, political, legal, and intellectual constraints they faced might be very different, but their perceptions of right and wrong were mutually comprehensible and, in the final analysis, shared. Reggie's article on the Berkeley faculty and the Free Speech Movement is called "On the Side of the Angels," and one of the titles he considered for his biography of Pankratova is "Neither Devil nor Angel." There are no angels and no devils in Reggie's work, but he usually knew whose side they were on, and he expected his subjects, colleagues, students, and friends to know, too, and to act accordingly. He did not expect perfection—he did not really like angels and he was not fascinated by devils— but he cared a great deal about the little decisions we all make as we "maneuver," along with Pankratova, in our perilous, "messy" worlds. His generosity was always equal to his "intellectual and moral certainty," and he never failed to notice the slightest tilt in the right direction. Was Pankratova a careerist, opportunist, ruthless crusader, and rigid ideologue? She was, in a way and at various times, "but it is my contention," writes Reggie, "that such negative characteristics take on a different shape when viewed in their historical and human contexts, when we stand closer to the object of study and watch her making the choices she had or didn't have to make."

Reggie stood very close to his objects of study—and to the rest of us, as well. He saw how, at the Nevsky trial, "even the police officers who testified for the prosecution seemed to take pains to present a fair picture of the defendants' behavior"; how Vasilii Gerasimov "made the best" of his "limited . . . but surprisingly varied" resources; how Governor Shakhovskoi tried to serve the law while being "trapped by circumstance somewhere between" two different conceptions of legality; and how, in "troubled and uncertain times," the Berkeley faculty struggled to find their way "in the gray area between procedure and substance."[17]

Whatever Mikhail Gorbachev's mistakes or even crimes, wrote Reggie in a 1991 article, "is it too much to ask that we praise a man who, however clumsily, confusedly, and without analytical elegance, 'tacked' . . . to the left, then to the right, then to the left . . . ? One sometimes needs this kind of a sailor in a storm."[18] And whatever Anna Pankratova's mistakes or even crimes, wrote Reggie in the conclusion to his last essay, is it too much to ask that we "imagine her as neither devil nor angel, as someone who did some harm but also much good as she tried to steer a course through the rough seas of Soviet life"?

We know it was not too much for Reggie. We know whose side he was on. We know there was no better sailor in any seas.

NOTES

All the unreferenced quotations in this paper are from *Perils of Pankratova*, in this volume.

1. I am grateful to Laura Engelstein, David Hollinger, Lisa Little, Benjamin Nathans, Amir Weiner, and Glennys Young for commenting on the manuscript; to Oksana Bulgakowa, George M. Enteen, and Norman M. Naimark for answering specific queries; to Miriam Neirick and Victoria Smolkin for help with research; and to Elaine and Pam Zelnik, for everything else.
2. A. M. Pankratova, ed., *Rabochee dvizhenie v Rossii v XIX veke. Sbornik dokumentov i materialov*, Vols. 1-4 (Moscow: Gospolitizdat, 1951-1963); Reginald E. Zelnik, "The Sunday-School Movement in Russia, 1859-1862," *Journal of Modern History*, Vol. 37, No. 2 (June 1965), pp. 151-170.
3. Reginald E. Zelnik, *A Radical Worker in Tsarist Russia: The Autobiography of Semën Ivanovich Kanatchikov* (Stanford, CA: Stanford University Press, 1986), pp. xviii, xxi-xxii.
4. Reginald E. Zelnik, ed., *Workers and Intelligentsia in Late Imperial Russia: Realities, Representations, Reflections* (Berkeley: International and Area Studies, University of California at Berkeley, 1999), pp. 40, 43.
5. Reginald E. Zelnik, "Prodigal Fathers and Existential Sons: A Report from Berkeley," *Dissent*, May-June 1966, p. 288.
6. Zelnik, *A Radical Worker*, p. xxx.
7. Reginald E. Zelnik, "The Fate of the Russian Bebel: Semën Ivanovich Kanatchikov,

1905-1940," in *The Carl Beck Papers in Russian and East European Studies*, No. 1105 (1995), p. 11.

8. Reginald E. Zelnik, *Law and Disorder on the Narova River: The Kreenholm Strike of 1872* (Berkeley and Los Angeles: University of California Press, 1995), pp. 1, 2, 269; Zelnik, *A Radical Worker*, pp. xv, xvi.

9. Zelnik, *Law and Disorder*, p. 7.

10. Reginald E. Zelnik, *Labor and Society in Tsarist Russia: The Factory Workers of St. Petersburg 1855-1870* (Stanford, CA: Stanford University Press, 1971).

11. Zelnik, *Law and Disorder*, pp. 1-2 and passim.

12. Reginald E. Zelnik, "On the Side of the Angels: The Berkeley Faculty and the FSM," in Robert Cohen and Reginald E. Zelnik, eds., *The Free Speech Movement: Reflections on Berkeley in the 1960s* (Berkeley and Los Angeles: University of California Press, 2002), pp. 264-338.

13. Reginald E. Zelnik, "Mario Savio: Avatar of Free Speech," in Cohen and Zelnik, *The Free Speech Movement*, p. 569; Reginald E. Zelnik, "Two Cheers for Gorbachev," *Tikkun*, Vol. 6, No. 6 (November-December 1991), p. 22.

14. Zelnik, "On the Side of the Angels," p. 264.

15. Reginald E. Zelnik, "Worry about Workers: Concerns of the Russian Intelligentsia from the 1870s to *What Is to Be Done?*" in Marsha Siefert, ed., *Extending the Borders of Russian History: Essays in Honor of Alfred J. Rieber* (Budapest: Central European University Press, 2003), p. 206.

16. Zelnik, "On the Side of the Angels," pp. 264-265; Zelnik, *Law and Disorder*, pp. 227 and 268; Reginald E. Zelnik, "Russian Bebels: An Introduction to the Memoirs of the Russian Workers Semën Kanatchikov and Matvei Fisher," *Russian Review*, Vol. 35, No. 3 (July 1976), pp. 288-289; Zelnik, *A Radical Worker*, p. xxx.

17. Zelnik, *Labor and Society in Tsarist Russia*, p. 355; Zelnik, *Law and Disorder*, pp. 269, 219; Zelnik, "On the Side of the Angels," pp. 264, 283.

18. Zelnik, "Two Cheers for Gorbachev," pp. 88-89.

PERILS OF PANKRATOVA:
Some Stories from the Annals of Soviet Historiography

Reginald E. Zelnik
Prepared for publication by Yuri Slezkine

Vernaia doch' kommunisticheskoi partii, ona posviatila vsiu svoiu zhizn' bor'be za torzhestvo leninizma[a]
— *Pravda* 29 May 1957 (Pankratova obituary)

Konkretnye primery ubezhdaiut, chto prioritet nauchnosti byl neosporim dlia mnogikh uchenykh, khotia ob etom malo govorilos' publichno[b]
— Liubov' Alekseevna Sidorova,
(historian, friend of Pankratova), 1997

AT LEAST UNTIL HER DEATH IN 1957, Anna Pankratova was indisputably the most important single contributor to the study of Russian labor history of the twentieth century. She was also one of the most powerful members of the Soviet Union's historical profession—to some degree a kingmaker (and unmaker)—but, like so many other Soviet academic leaders, someone who was always vulnerable to dethronement herself. Not untypically, during her professional career she was dethroned and restored more than once. My purpose in this paper, which is based on a combination of published primary and secondary sources, is not to make a definitive assessment of her very complicated career, but to take us on a tour through the high points (or low points) of the muddy, messy world of Soviet historiography as exemplified by Pankratova's professional and political life. (Because of her proudly proclaimed *partiinost'*,[c] the two are of course hard to separate). Although much has been published in Russia about her since her death, until the appearance of a rich collection of memoirs, analyses,

---

a. "A loyal daughter of the Communist Party, she devoted her whole life to the struggle for the triumph of Leninism."
b. "Specific examples demonstrate that for many scholars, true scholarship was the ultimate value, even though it was not customary to say so in public."
c. "Party spirit," "Party-mindedness."

and archival documents in the year 2000, access to most of the published material was weighed down by the constraints of Soviet censorship and self-censorship as well as by post-Soviet delicacy.[1] This new collection, while not totally devoid of the latter problem, allows us to look more closely and with greater accuracy at the more controversial moments of Pankratova's very troubled yet in its own way creative life. One question that I wish to raise in this paper, though I will not address it directly until the very end (and then only briefly), is simply: How should we be talking about a life like Pankratova's? What is the appropriate language for historians to use, and what should be the role of moral assessment in an analysis of this kind of life?

Anna Mikhailovna Pankratova was born in the bustling port city of Odessa in February 1897.[2] She was a child of the working class if ever there was one. Her father, Mikhail Fedorovich, was a factory worker of peasant background, probably the son of serfs, who had left his Kaluga village to seek work in Odessa. Her mother, Elizaveta Nikiforovna, a peasant from Saratov province, took in laundry and did other kinds of menial day labor to help keep the family afloat, especially after the death in 1906 of the father, who had been seriously wounded in combat in the Russo-Japanese War. Since Mikhail died when she was only nine, and her mother was sickly, Anna (who was also called Niura), the oldest of four children, spent much of her Odessa youth struggling to support her family while attending school. Her primary occupation, assisted by her siblings, was to cut the long strands of wick she brought home from a candlewick factory, and to thread them into the tin crosses used for icon-lamps. After completing a *narodnaia shkola*[d] with decent grades, Anna won a state stipend to a local *gimnaziia* for girls, where her performance was good enough to land her a prestigious Leo Tolstoy scholarship. Around 1912 she began to live apart from her family, which she continued to help by working in a small factory and doing tutorial work, her first modest exposure to the role of teacher. Anna graduated from the *gimnaziia* with a gold medal in 1914, just on the eve of the war, and then enrolled as a *kursistka*[e] in the History section of the Historical-Philosophical Faculty of Odessa's newly established college-level school for women (the *Vysshie zhenskie*

---

d. primary school.
e. female student.

kursy), which merged with the Novorossiiski University in academic year 1916-17. As her daughter Maia would later put it, Anna studied history from the textbooks that future Soviet historians (Anna among them) would later disdainfully label "bourgeois."[3] While working as a part-time teacher, including at evening classes for workers, Pankratova completed all or most of her course work, though not her exit exams or thesis (*diplom-naia rabota*), in 1917, when, like so many other students, *kursistki* among them, she interrupted her studies to devote her full time to the revolutionary cause, a cause she never really left.

Attracted as were so many youths of her background—in nine-teenth-century terms, one might think of her as a young *raznochinnaia intelligentka*[4,f]—to radical politics, Anna threw in her lot with the local Socialist-Revolutionary Party in 1917, supporting its "internationalist" wing and devoting herself to political-educational work (i.e., propaganda) among the workers, students, and especially peasants of Odessa *uezd*. Like many Left SRs, she rallied to the October Revolution, but, unlike many of them, when their final break with the Bolsheviks took place in summer 1918 she hitched her wagon to the Bolshevik cause, joining the Party offi-cially in February of the following year. Since at various times during the Civil War Odessa was in the hands of the Bolsheviks' enemies, including the German and Austrian armies, French expeditionary forces, and Denikin's army, Anna's political work in the region was mainly in the underground, where she assumed the nom de guerre of "Niura Palich" and spent part of her time undercover as a waitress in a dairy bar. Although she was of Great Russian nationality on both sides, growing up in Odessa and participating in its multi-ethnic, often Jewish radical milieu—in 1919 she briefly served as secretary of the Party Committee of Odessa's heavily Jewish Moldavanka district—exposed her to a social environment that can truly be described as "cosmopolitan," a term that would come back to haunt some of her closest comrades half a century later.[5]

As an energetic and committed young Bolshevik whose political iden-tity was honed in social and military conflict, Anna learned early on to take her orders from her Party superiors. Among her main *komandirovki*,[g] beginning in 1920, was an extended (nearly two-year) assignment to the Ural Region, where she served, inter alia, as secretary of the regional com-

---

f. intelligentsia member of non-gentry origin.
g. assignments involving travel.

14

mittee (*raikom*) of the metalworkers union and engaged in propaganda and other political-educational work in the region's metallurgical industry. During the same years she was also dispatched by the Party to Kharkov and other venues and was assigned such important Party responsibilities as secretary of various *raikomy, obkomy,* and *gubkomy,*[h] and assistant chief of the Party's Women's Section (*zhenotdel*) in Odessa, appointments at the age of 23 and 24 that reflected her talents and energy as well as the shortage of reliable personnel with the requisite political and social credentials. The combination of Anna's personal experience, her own background, her ready access to factory archives in the Urals, and her professional academic aspirations carved out her career path and helped launch her vocation as a specialist in the young field of working-class history. This professional choice was of course a political choice as well, and the institutions where she would now receive her professional training—most notably the Institute of Red Professors (IKP, founded in early 1921), which functioned under the aegis of the Agitprop section of the Central Committee of the Party (hereafter, TsK)—were as political as could be. Pankratova asked for and received a delay in order to prepare for the Institute's entrance examinations, which she then passed, though not brilliantly. Given her social origins, class background, and political qualifications (though a Party *stazh*[i] dating to 1919 was not nearly as valuable at the time as one dating to 1917 or earlier), she certainly had the earmarks of the kind of young woman whom the Party hoped to shape into a new kind of Communist person (*novyi chelovek*) by means of special education at such new institutions as the IKP, the Sverdlov Academy, and the Communist Academy.[6]

At the IKP, which she graduated in 1925, and during academic year 1926-27, which she spent with other *ikapisty* (IKP graduates) at the Leningrad branch of the Institute of History (LOII) on a mission to counteract the influence of non-Marxist scholars, Pankratova had close encounters with both an older generation of "bourgeois" historians (among them Evgenii Tarle, Boris Grekov, Aleksandr Presniakov, and Iurii Got'e), a younger generation of aspiring young Marxists like herself, and a small number of seasoned Marxists from the older generation. Of the senior Marxists in Moscow, the most influential, of course, was the ill-fated Communist Mikhail Pokrovskii, who headed the IKP's History

---

h. Party committees at various administrative levels.
i. length of service.

faculty and for the time being enjoyed enormous influence and prestige.

Pokrovskii, whose links to pre-Revolutionary historiography included a not very happy apprenticeship with Vasilii Kliuchevskii,[7] was without a doubt the main formative influence on Pankratova the historian, though one that she would eventually live to regret, at least in public. Pokrovskii quickly took to the bright, industrious, newly minted *kommunistka*[j] and virtually adopted her as his disciple, his "right hand," as one historian has put it.[8] Under his protection, Pankratova, still only in her mid-twenties, soon became a leader of the *ikapisty* and a driving force in the new field of Russian labor history, to which she helped give its initial form and direction and which she continued to shape and influence almost until her death. By 1925 she had already published three books and numerous articles in this field, the most noteworthy being her history of Russia's factory committees (*fabzavkomy*) and their role in the recent revolutionary saga. The book, edited by Pokrovskii, was partially based on Pankratova's work in the archives of the Ural *zavody*.[9,k] She also published a much less thorough monograph on comparable developments in Western Europe, especially the factory councils or sovety (*Räte*) of post-war Germany, where she spent a scant two months gathering materials in 1926.[10]

After completing her graduate work in 1925, Pankratova, by now very much under Pokrovskii's wing, devoted herself for the next few years to the history of Russia's labor unions and to the role of workers in the 1905 Revolution, research that culminated in a series of reports and articles that appeared in 1929 and 1930 in conjunction with the celebration of that revolution's twenty-fifth anniversary. But her research time suffered from her various teaching assignments, most of which she seems to have welcomed, and from a wide range of exhausting political, organizational, and editorial duties, some of which she probably did not. These efforts came together in her powerful ambition to organize and oversee the massive publication of documents and monographs on Russian labor history, works usually edited by a "collective" of scholars headed by herself. This was an impressive accomplishment, especially when one considers that almost her entire adult life was plagued by serious illness, political strife, and the triple burden of single-motherhood, mothering her nieces, and caring for an ailing mother of her own (though one who managed to outlive her).[11]

---

j. female Communist.
k. factories.

16

Pankratova's single-motherhood began in 1927, when her private life (if one can even use such a term) suffered an enormous blow in the form of her first personal experience of the full-scale Communist oppression of Communists.[1] In that year Pankratova was forced to confront the frightening news that her husband, Grigorii Iakovin, a fellow *ikapist* and fellow Communist, a specialist in German history, was denounced as a supporter of Trotsky and the Left Opposition and was arrested and exiled to Tashkent for his political sins. Faced with the agonizing choice of following her husband into exile and disgrace or actively and publicly breaking her ties to him—by the end of the 1920s it was really all or nothing— Pankratova chose the latter course. (As far as I know, she would never remarry.) Pankratova's own version of this personal tragedy—as recounted, to be sure, in the extreme conditions of 1936, when the IKP's Party group was considering her expulsion—is worth quoting for the light it sheds on the mood of the times (and on Iakovin's evident refusal to repent):

> [After speaking out against my husband in 1927] I broke off with him and asked for leave. . . . . In 1929 I had the idea that I would influence Iakovin [to change his ideas]. . . . I went to Tashkent where Iakovin was in prison. I lived with him in a hotel for 3-4 days, but after [our] discussions [*beseda*] I saw that we were enemies [*liudi vrazhdebnye*], so I broke off my connection with my husband. In 1933 he sent a letter to our daughter and a note to me with a request that he [be allowed to] correspond with his daughter. I responded with a question: what were his current political views [*na kakikh pozitsiiakh on stoit*]? I passionately [*uzhasno*] hoped that he was not a Trotskyist [any longer]. Not because of my personal life, but so that my daughter would not have a Trotskyist-father [*otets trotskist*].[12]

We can only begin to imagine the actual content of the couple's three-day "*beseda.*"

Still in the Party's good graces following her 1927 denunciation of her husband, but of course with the shadow of his deviation now hovering over her, Pankratova remained in Moscow with her daughter Maia, who henceforth bore her mother's last name, while retaining her patronymic, Grigor'evna. Pankratova's rejection of a husband whom, at least according

---

1. Pankratova had a daughter, Maia Pankratova.

17

to her daughter, she really loved,[13] her subordination of personal ties to Party loyalties, anticipated many similar painful choices for her and people like her in the years ahead.

Pankratova's personal difficulties were inevitably accompanied by and entangled in challenges of a political nature, which began as early as 1924, if not earlier. As Michael David-Fox has shown us, in the 1920s the IKP itself was often the scene of major purges and orchestrated hunts for "deviationists"—"left" in the mid-1920s, "right" in 1928-1929—and for "nationalists," both Russian and "other."[14] In addition, Pankratova found herself in numerous conflict situations that boiled up during her sojourn in Leningrad in 1926-1927. Pokrovskii had sent her (accompanied by her still untainted husband) and her comrade and fellow *ikapist* G. S. Zaidel', also a Pokrovskii student,[15] on a year-long mission to Leningrad to monitor the non-Marxist historians who in Pokrovskii's view enjoyed an excessive influence on the scholarly life in that city, most notably Presniakov and Tarle, whose superficial and inadequate veneer of Marxism Pokrovskii belittled and even despised.[16] Pankratova and Zaidel' were also instructed to mentor the youngest generation of Marxist scholars and help organize a politically acceptable historical research institute at Leningrad State University (LGU), to serve as the Leningrad branch of the Institute of History (centrally located in Moscow).[17] In the 1920s Tarle enjoyed the great esteem of some of the brightest and most independent young Leningrad historians, as did the venerable Sergei Platonov (though unlike Tarle, Platonov preferred to hold himself aloof from his students and junior colleagues).[18] Despite Pokrovskii's burgeoning campaign to box in Tarle and place all historical scholarship in the iron grip of Soviet Marxism, a campaign in which Pankratova was expected to play an important part, compared to the form they took two years later the ensuing conflicts were relatively restrained, part of what Konstantine Shteppa has described as an ongoing trench warfare that preserved a precarious "equilibrium" or "coexistence" between old and new until it began to spin out of control in 1928-1929 and then was harshly resolved in favor of the "new" (or *some* of the new) in the so-called "Akademicheskoe delo" of 1929-1931.[19]

In the spring of 1927 the thirty-year-old Pankratova, who still held no professorship and was for the moment lacking in clear directives from Moscow (Pokrovskii was very ill at the time), modestly declined full membership and a leadership role in the LOII, which, as she indicated, would have placed her on a par with such luminaries as Tarle, Presniakov, and Grekov. Despite pressures from Pokrovskii and the willingness of Presniakov, who was less hostile to Marxism than some of his colleagues, she correctly insisted and publicly declared that she had not yet earned such a post on her academic merits. But the ailing Pokrovskii, often at dagger's point with Tarle and his colleagues, would not take "no" for an answer, and both she and Zaidel' were prematurely elevated to the status of full members. This was Pokrovskii's doing, and not Pankratova's. At this still early stage of the conflicts between the "bourgeois professoriate" and the new political establishment, which at this point were as much about personnel appointments and staffing as they were about well-artic-ulated historical or ideological issues, Pankratova and Zaidel' generally tried to take a moderating position and were solicitous of the older historians' feelings, especially Tarle's.[20]

It was not long, however, before Russia's "bourgeois" historians and archivists began to undergo the severe political repression of the Akademicheskoe delo. Among those purged from their academic positions and arrested in 1929-1931 (mainly 1930) and charged with offenses such as monarchism, white-guardism, concealment of counterrevolutionary documents, and plotting with exiled Russian, French, German, Polish, and Vatican conspirators to overthrow the Soviet regime, were senior scholars such as the full Academicians Platonov, Tarle, Nikolai Likhachev, and Matvei Liubavskii as well as several corresponding members of the Academy, including Presniakov and Iurii Got'e. (Presniakov, one of Platonov's star students, might well have been among them had he not died of cancer in September 1929, shortly before the first arrests.[21]) But less prominent historians such as Nikolai Druzhinin, though by now for many years a devotee of the Communist cause, were absurdly accused of plotting to restore the tsarist regime as well.[22] Younger historians and archivists were also victimized if there was reason to believe they were associated with people like Tarle.[23]

In 1930 Pankratova herself barely escaped the dragnet when she was charged by members of her Party cell in the Vysshaia shkola profdvizheniia (VShPD) with excessive sympathy for one of the VShPD's former members, the purged "Trotskyite" historian V. Iarotskii. That accusation may have gained credibility because of her recent marital history, but it was based on Pankratova's actual attempts to come to Iarotskii's defense. At the same time, a time when Stalin's followers were able to speak without embarrassment of the dangers of the "right-left bloc," it should also come as no surprise that members of her IKP Party cell also accused her of *right* deviation. None of these accusations was directly related to the Akademicheskoe delo, but they did reflect the general repressiveness that was casting its shadow over the academic world at the beginning of the decade, as it was on so many other aspects of Russian life. Pankratova was lucky in the sense that, as was true of several other scholars from her milieu, the primary accusation against her was less the harboring of unacceptable deviationist ideas herself than excessive softness toward those who did. She was also fortunate in that this was still a time when exoneration was not unusual. That Pokrovskii came vigorously to her defense was still a plus, and may explain why some members of the Central Committee eventually intervened in her behalf. After considerable delay and uncertainty, her case was finally heard by a Troika of the Central Control Commission of the Worker-Peasant Inspection, which ruled on 5 December 1930 that because she had not *supported* Iarotskii's "errors" but had merely asked that he be kept in the Party *despite* those errors, her actions did not justify her own expulsion or other serious punishment; hence her accusers in the VPShD's Party cell—had they been playing out their parts in the "cultural revolution"?—were found to have acted irresponsibly by "casting a shadow" on her political conduct.[24]

To be sure, accusations of softness toward her non-Marxist colleagues were serious charges, to the extent that in early 1931 Pokrovskii, having acted as her protector, referred to her case as the "so-called *delo Pankratovoi*"[m] and was still so fearful of the effect of her "persecution" (*travlia*) on her health that he turned to Viacheslav Molotov for assistance.[25] The episode, which dragged on for many months, contributed to another breakdown in Pankratova's physical and mental well-being, even causing her hospitalization.[26] Yet compared to others, she emerged relatively unscathed from this wave of repression, perhaps a sign of her willingness to play the Party's game, at least verbally. It should be noted, however, that in contrast to her comrade Zaidel', who played a disreputable role as "expert" witness and OGPU "consultant" in the Akademicheskoe delo, she does not seem to have been used in that manner.[27]

Despite her troubles, setbacks, and one near miss, Pankratova's professional star generally continued to rise in these years, marked by her

---

m. Pankratova affair.

ascendancy in the 1930s as the Soviet Union's most recognized authority in the field of labor history. As of 1928, under Pokrovskii's nominal supervision, she had run the Society of Marxist Historians' newly created Commission for the Study of the Russian Proletariat, and at the very important first conference of that society (December 1928 - January 1929), an event that helped seal the fate of some of the old generation of historians, Pankratova gave the definitive agenda-setting report on "The Problem of Studying the Working Class in Russia."[28] Some months later she was finally named Professor at Moscow University (MGU), and in 1935, notwithstanding the *delo Pankratovoi*, the exonerated professor was placed in charge of the university's newly formed History *kafedra*.[n] But by then she was compelled to cope with the even more explosive *delo Pokrovskogo*.[o]

It should probably come as no surprise that, having turned her back on her husband, Pankratova would prove herself capable of turning against her doctor-father, though not without considerable hesitation. Intense attacks on Pokrovskii by the influential Communist historian Emel'ian Iaroslavskii and others were already detectable in 1929-1930,[29] well before Pokrovskii's death from bladder cancer in 1932, and their intensification may already have been conceived at the time of Stalin's infamous letter to the editors of *Proletarskaia revoliutsiia* in the fall of 1931. They began to take on more steam in the years that followed, escalated after Stalin's—they were also Kirov's and Zhdanov's—1934 "Observations" (*Zamechaniia*) on the proper teaching of history, and crystallized fully by late 1936, the time of the launching of the Great Terror. By then Pokrovskii and his "school" were being fiercely denounced for a host of deviations and "pseudo-Marxist" errors, including his excessively abstract, lifeless, and faceless economic determinism (an orientation he had in fact begun to criticize himself in the late 1920s[30]). Led by Iaroslavskii, dozens of Soviet scholars viciously maligned the former megastar of their profession and, whatever one may think of Pokrovskii's uneven scholarship, horribly distorted his professional and personal record, describing him as a "wrecker" and piling on many other ugly epithets. This anti-Pokrovskii campaign is by now a story told many times

---

n. program or field within an academic department.
o. Pokrovskii affair.

over, and needs no retelling here, but Pankratova's special role calls for additional comment.

Perhaps because she still lived in the shadow of her husband's never-to-be-forgotten Trotskyism and the subsequent challenge to her political integrity by her Party cell in 1930, but especially because of her very special close relationship with Pokrovskii for almost a decade, it may have been inevitable that Pankratova would eventually be required to be "more Catholic than the Pope" in the sweep of her denunciations. Nevertheless, in order to be adequately shocked by what ultimately became her leading role in the attacks on Pokrovskii, one needs to be reminded of the great devotion to her mentor that Pankratova had expressed in the quite recent past. In 1928, for example, she had written to him in language that surely went beyond mere academic formality: "At the present time the dream and goal of my life is to write the kind of serious scholarly work that I would have the right to dedicate to you—my first and only teacher and guide [rukovoditel'] in the area of historical scholarship"; she signed off—"With deep esteem and love for you" (S glubokym uvazheniem i liubov'iu k Vam).[31] Her correspondence with Pokrovskii right up to the eve of his death is replete with requests for advice, complaints about her illnesses and excessive workload (another constant, lifetime theme in her correspondence), and expressions of extreme concern about his failing health. In January 1932, when Pokrovskii was approaching his death, Pankratova was writing to him in the warmest terms (though always na Vy[p]) and wishing him well,[32] and as late as early 1934, when others were sharpening their anti-Pokrovskii swords, she could still praise her former mentor in the pages of Vestnik Kommunisticheskoi Akademii as a true "pupil of Lenin,[33] even while she began to re-embrace "bourgeois" historians like Tarle, now in his period of "semi-rehabilitation." (Back from exile in Alma-Ata, partially restored to the regime's good graces, his "plan" to overthrow the government apparently forgotten, if not forgiven, Tarle was tenderly addressing Pankratova as "Annushka.")[34]

Thereafter Pankratova became more careful, and for very good reason. In the burgeoning terror of 1936-37, several of her closest professional colleagues, including such past Communist stalwarts as Academicians David Riazanov and Nikolai Lukin (Nikolai Bukharin's

---

p. Polite form of address, analogous to the French "vous," German "Sie," and Spanish "Usted."

Anna Mikhailovna Pankratova.
From V. V. Al'tman, ed., *Iz istorii rabochego klassa i revoliutsionnogo dvizheniia* (Moscow: Akademiia nauk SSSR, 1958).

brother-in-law) and Pankratova's comrade, co-worker, and former OGPU "consultant" and defamer of Tarle, Zaidel', were interrogated, dismissed from the Party, imprisoned, and worse.[35] Pankratova's modest vacation home in Otdykh, a little settlement of dachas outside of Moscow where she and her family spent much of their leisure time, quickly emptied out: "There was not a single house from which people didn't disappear," including the editor of *Izvestiia*, with whom Pankratova shared her dacha, as well as the two IKP employees whose dachas abutted hers.[36] In August 1936, in Moscow, where her similarly harassed colleague Arkadii Sidorov found her looking "dark and exhausted,"[37] Pankratova herself was grilled by the Party collective of her own beloved IKP and charged by her colleagues with having defended and protected the "counterrevolutionary Trotskyist" *ikapisty* Zaidel' and Vanag. She was soon expelled from the Party, after which she was dismissed from her MGU professorship in the spring of 1937 and was exiled to Saratov, her mother's home province.[38]

Under these circumstances, with her former colleagues disappearing all around her, Pankratova kept as cautious a distance as she could from the public debate over Pokrovskii. Not surprisingly, though permitted to teach at Saratov State University, she published almost nothing at all in 1936-38—two minor articles in 1936 and nothing for the next two years, the only such barren years in her professional life.[39] But by this time Pokrovskii and his "school" had been officially condemned by the TsK itself, and in no uncertain terms, leaving the exiled Pankratova with little room for maneuver. By 1938 she had joined the loud chorus of those who were vigorously denouncing her former mentor, with what degree of conviction we may never know. Her Party membership restored, she now agreed to serve as a major editor and contributor to the two main volumes of implausible anti-Pokrovskii diatribes that appeared in 1939 and 1940, volumes that continue to be associated with her name.[40]

The sincerity of Pankratova's attacks on her former mentor and protector can never be ascertained with any precision, and, posed in those terms, it may not even be an answerable question. One can only guess if she would have had the temerity to go as far as she did had Pokrovskii still been alive, though in this case it is hard to give her the benefit of the doubt. Nevertheless, two very personal letters by Pankratova recently discovered in the archives by A. N. Artizova can help us to reconstruct aspects of Pankratova's state of mind in 1937, as she faced her own mortality and contemplated the ominous events that surrounded her.[41]

Pankratova's correspondent, Elena Kirillovna Sokolovskaia (addressed in both letters as "Rodnaia Lenochka!"[q]), then the well-known artistic director of Mosfilm, was perhaps her closest friend and confidant. The two young women had been co-conspirators during the Civil War years in Odessa's revolutionary underground, of which Sokolovskaia was a renowned and much admired leader.[42] The first letter, dated 6 March 1937, was written at a time when Pankratova, by then under siege by Party organizations for six "unbelievably terrifying" (*nepostizhimo strashnye*) months, was still uncertain of what horrors might befall her. Though advised by a member of the Party Control Commission that her penalty might be confined to the relatively mild one of expulsion from the Party for a year and a term of exile to the provinces, Pankratova was well aware of the severe punishments being meted out to many of her former colleagues and comrades. She therefore wrote her letter "in the anguish [*toska*] of anticipation of my coming fate" (which she correctly expected to learn after the forthcoming TsK plenum), although, as she had already told her friend by telephone, she was "prepared to submit to any decision of the party, without the slightest murmur."[43]

However great her fear for her own future, it did not prevent Pankratova from expressing joy and enthusiasm about her girlhood friend's latest professional "triumph," the creation of the "remarkable

---

q. "Dearest Lenochka" ("Lenochka" is an affectionate diminutive for "Elena").

Bolshevik film" *Posledniaia noch*ʳ (directed by the popular Iulii Raizman), made in honor of the twentieth anniversary of the Bolshevik Revolution: "You know that I very much love the cinema, as the most powerful instrument for the education of millions. And how happy I am that that instrument is located in your good hands!" As some of these words suggest, Pankratova's letter was replete with assertions of her continued *partiinost'*, her unwavering devotion, despite all the attendant circumstances, not only to the socialist cause in general, not only to "our socialist art," as she put it, but to the Communist Party in particular. "Surely and irrevocably," she wrote, "there is one thing I know: I have never, whether by word, deed, or thought, deceived the Party or my friends, [and I have] devoted all my life and all my strength to the party and the revolution."⁴⁴ If she was now in trouble, it was not because of her own disloyalty, but because of her one admitted "defect" (*porok*), an excess of credulousness and liberalism, a weakness that allowed the devious people who had at times surrounded her (Zaidel'? Vanag? Pokrovskii? her husband?) to count on her trust and protection; it was her tendency to love and to pity even the undeserving, her refusal, until recently, to hate even the enemy, she explained, that had repeatedly done her in. Yet she still prided herself for having overcome her weakness, for having survived a sojourn in a mental hospital, and for having become morally "stronger," thanks to her determined effort to "mobilize all her strength, all her will" while awaiting the verification of the charges against her.⁴⁵ She then concluded her letter to Lenochka with these words: "At any time, at any place, whatever may happen to me, I will be and will remain an honest person, completely [*do kontsa*] committed to the party, ready to devote my entire life to the cause of socialism. It seems likely that I will soon be going away for a long time. Will I have a chance to take leave of you?"⁴⁶

The second letter, dated 11 May 1937, was sent from Saratov in response to what was apparently a warmly worded telegram from Lenochka, one that revived the exiled historian's will to live at a time when her other "comrades" had let her down.⁴⁷ Having learned that Sokolovskaia still believed in her, extended her hand to her, even while Pankratova "was hanging over an abyss" (*povisla nad bezdnoi*), she now declared her capacity to recoup the moral and physical strength that she needed to devote herself to "our motherland." Specifically, she assured

---

r. "The last night."

Sokolovskaia that she was eagerly bending every effort to fulfill her new pedagogical tasks in Saratov, an important center of academic life. Relieved, no doubt, that her penalty had not involved a term in a Siberian camp or worse, Pankratova was "deeply and sincerely thankful to the party," and especially to the Control Commission, for having sent her to work in the provinces, where she was now closer to "the masses" and where she hoped to demonstrate with time that she was worthy of reinstatement. "Lenochka," she continued,

> this is a new phase of my life, of my struggle for a new spiritual and physical existence [*za novuiu zhizn' dukha i tela*]. I have lost a lot, but the most important thing has remained: an indestructible faith and unshakeable desire, together with the entire country and the party, to complete the job of building socialism [*dovesti do kontsa delo sotsializma*]. I have understood my great errors and felt them deeply. But they were not [the products] of any malicious intent and desire. I have never broken with the party in any way. And [she accurately predicted] I will stay with the party for the rest of my life.

Although it was clear that he was among the people Pankratova regretted once having placed too much trust in, there was only one direct reference to Pokrovskii in the letters. In the second letter, she proudly announced that she had recently subjected to "a serious self-critical reexamination," those "views, concepts, and schemes" that had dominated the Soviet history field under the influence of Pokrovskii's "school," that is, those views, concepts, and schemes that she had so admired until quite recently. Since April, she explained, she had been criticizing those views in a series of well-received lectures to the youth of Saratov, and more such lectures were scheduled for May. It is likely that this reexamination and these lectures provided a foundation for the attacks on Pokrovskii she would publish in 1939 and 1940.

Although sincerity is always a tough issue to address, there is little reason to doubt Pankratova's avowals of devotion to the Party, socialism, and the revolutionary cause, all of which she conflated into a single profession of Communist faith. She was, after all, writing in intimate terms to a very dear friend. While one cannot rule out that she hoped that the letters would be read by Party censors and would thereby work in her favor, it seems probable that the letters were not sent through the mail but hand-delivered by a mutual friend. Moreover, if the letters were intended for official perusal, even a routine statement in praise of Stalin would have helped her cause, as would a more robust, direct, and extensive denunciation of Pokrovskii, yet both were absent. One might even read some qualms about Stalin in the complete absence of his name, even in Pankratova's litany of synonyms for the cause to which she was so devoted. Nor did her profession of faith require her to include the kind of vigorous self-criticism that was so common at the time, excessive credulousness and generosity (roughly the same crimes of which she had been accused five years earlier) hardly being comparable to counterrevolutionary espionage, treason, or wrecking. Admitting to a minimum of guilt with perhaps a maximum of zeal, Pankratova was preparing herself for reinstatement in a political institution that had been her permanent home for almost her entire adult life and in a profession to which she was entirely devoted. If this was opportunism, it was the kind of opportunism that required little in the way of either soul-searching or complex ratiocination. Pankratova was by now hard-wired to think, feel, and speak quite "naturally" in the terms she now used in her letters to her friend,[48] the only exception, the most likely area to have involved a more garden-variety kind of opportunism, being her unexplained (and perhaps academically inexplicable) and seemingly ritual wholesale dismissal of the approach to history she had nominally espoused throughout her professional apprenticeship with Pokrovskii.

Pankratova's published attacks on Pokrovskii in 1938-1940 should perhaps be viewed as a form of penance, though one about which she clearly had little choice if she wanted to survive. Writing as a survivor of the Terror, as Pokrovskii's premier protégée, as the ex-wife of a condemned Trotskyite, as the accused protector of "counterrevolutionaries," and as a former Left SR, she was a pretty likely candidate for the GULAG and/or execution (though actuarially less vulnerable than if she had qualified as a genuine pre-October "Old Bolshevik," especially a male). She was lucky to have gotten by with exile to Saratov where, much like many a political exile to that town in tsarist times, she was permitted to carry on with what in those daunting days passed for a fairly normal intellectual and professional life, not to mention a home life with her daughter and mother. For nearly three years Pankratova held a professorship at the recently established (1935) History Faculty of Saratov State University, where in 1939 she even became the department head. Throughout these years of exile, she was also allowed to maintain her affiliation with the Institute of History in Moscow and even to visit that city from time to time. Perhaps she saw her denunciations of a dead man's scholarship as a small price to pay for this relative good fortune.[49] After a suspension of less than two years, Pankratova was readmitted to the Party in 1938, the very year when Lenochka, her dear friend, supporter, and correspondent, was sentenced to death.[50] In 1939, her last year of exile, Pankratova's rehabilitation took an additional step forward: she was named a corresponding member of the Academy of Sciences.[51]

The mid- and late 1930s were not the best years for Russian labor history, a field that Pokrovskii had encouraged since the late 1920s and that Pankratova had been dominating at least since 1928-29, when she and Pokrovskii turned "the history of the proletariat" into a major project of the Communist Academy's Institute of History and the Society of Marxist Historians.[52] Not only did many historians—among them some of Pankratova's scholarly collaborators—eventually fall victim to the terror, but also, beginning in 1934, Stalin's bending of the historical profession away from Pokrovskii's "lifeless" and "faceless" socioeconomic categories diminished the importance of social history, including the history of the working class. A premium was now placed on more colorful and personalized representations of the Russian national past, while class analysis as it had been practiced by Pokrovskii, Pankratova, and others, found itself on the back burner. Nevertheless, Pankratova was able to maintain her professional reputation and status as a labor historian by virtue of her deep involvement in an important project enthusiastically promoted by none other than Maxim Gorky—the very ambitious "factory history" project or *Istoriia fabrik i zavodov* SSSR (sometimes referred to simply as *Istfab* or as IFZ). Gorky's project, which led to the formation of a special commission under the aegis of the TsK itself, was aimed at a popular rather than an academic audience. The plan was to get real live production workers (but also technical specialists and *sluzhashchie*[s]) involved in both the writing and the reading of their own history, and to encourage good, broadly appealing popular writers rather than "dry" scholars to produce much of the prose.[53]

Pankratova, who in the 1920s had put so much time and energy into her pedagogical contacts with the workers of the Urals and other regions,

---

s. white-collar employees.

could not help but be attracted to the project and certainly had no basis to refuse Gorky's invitation to play a leading role on the commission. At the same time, as she told Pokrovskii, she had professional reservations about Gorky, and especially about his failure to invest the *Istfab* project with sufficient scholarly substance. "I'm afraid to be a prophet," she wrote him, "but I fear very much that this business could end up as a huge scandal, fraught with [bad] consequences. One should not farm out an enormous and extremely difficult undertaking like the history of factories to writers and essayists who have no concept of the methods of historical research."[54] Here she was referring to Gorky's view that writers of fiction (*belletristy*) should have a major role in the writing process—he and others, including, eventually, Pankratova, often used the qualifier *nauchno-populiarnyi*[t] when referring to the mixed genre that the project aimed at creating.

To emphasize this literary angle, Gorky unveiled his plan at a September 1931 plenary meeting of the militant Russian Association of Proletarian Writers (RAPP), still unaware that the organization would survive only seven more months. Paraphrasing Marx, he concluded his persuasive presentation to RAPP with the declaration that the publication of the history of factories was the "business of the workers themselves" (*delo samikh rabochikh*).[55] With the express approval of the TsK, perhaps necessitated by the warm afterglow of the *delo Pankratovoi*, Pankratova agreed to join the initial central editorial board (*Glavnaia redaktsiia*) of the new society. Suppressing her reservations, and perhaps her unhappiness that Gorky was, in effect, taking over a research plan that resembled a proposal that Pankratova had already initiated herself in 1928-30, she soon wrote an enthusiastic letter to Gorky, calling his *Istfab* project a "great cause." Nevertheless, she made it a point to let him know that she and her colleagues had already embarked on a similar project and had published a significant amount of material on the history of factories in the series *Istoriia proletariata SSSR*,[u] Pankratova's beloved "child" (*detishche*).[56]

Working on Gorky's factory history project became Pankratova's primary activity until her exile to Saratov. She had her hand in the preparation and publication of the numerous volumes—many of them multi-authored with real worker participation—published in the project's first few years. If some of these volumes—perhaps the most prominent among them was

---

t. "popular-scholarly"; that is, scholarly material aimed at the general reader.
u. *History of the Proletariat of the USSR.*

Zavod imeni Lenina, 1857-1918[v] (Moscow, 1933), by the former worker
N. P. Paialin—were the culmination of efforts begun under her sponsorship well before Gorky's brainstorm, Pankratova was willing (or perhaps
had no choice other than) to fold these earlier endeavors into Gorky's—
now really the TsK's—project. A European scholar listening to her effusive
1933 Warsaw report on the virtues of the project (or reading its pre-
Congress version published in German in the *Bulletin* of the International
Historians' Congress), including its innovative use of oral history, would
have been totally unaware of her initial reservations. Paying warm tribute
to Gorky's initiative, she presented the project as a unique product of the
Bolshevik Revolution, a contribution to the building of socialism and to
"socialist competition" among factories, and as the grandiose heroic
achievement of millions of workers, as such unattainable by scholars of the
less-advanced capitalist world. For the first time in human history, the
object of the study of history—the working class, the masses—had also
become its subject.[57] One might have thought the *Istoriia fabrik* the
Dneprostroi of historical scholarship.

Describing the factory history project to the "bourgeois historians" of
the West in 1933 provided Pankratova with a good opportunity to define
the current state of her thought regarding the issue of objectivity versus
political commitment in historical scholarship. One of the chief official
criticisms of Pokrovskii during the 1930s, noted repeatedly in Pankratova's
anti-Pokrovskii volumes, was his alleged dictum that history was present
politics projected on the past (*oprokinutaia v proshloe*). If Pankratova
rejected this formulation, however, her acclaim for the project left no
doubt that she continued to reject "objectivism" and to view scholarship
as always having a class perspective, with the best scholarship serving the
purposes of the Party and the working class. The project, she announced
unabashedly, had a "precise political goal": in studying the past, the masses
were to be mobilized to attain a better understanding of the present and to
struggle successfully for a better future. "For a Marxist," she continued,
"there is no such thing, nor can there be, as so-called objective scholarship
[*ob"ektivnaia nauka*], located beyond the goals and interests of a ruling
class. The aims of the revolutionary practice of the USSR's proletariat
determine the necessity of the *Istoriia zavodov* and account for its political
significance today [*politicheskaia aktual'nost'*]."[58]

---

v. *The Lenin Factory, 1857-1918.*

Preoccupation with the factory histories and their attendant travels, which involved virtually all industrial regions of the RSFSR and the Ukrainian Republic[59] (but almost no other parts of the Soviet Union), undoubtedly made it easier for Pankratova to keep at some distance from the ugly attacks on Pokrovskii that began to multiply in 1934, especially after the assassination of Kirov. To a great extent, the factory history project, despite its insistence on an accessible sequential narrative style that differed markedly from Pokrovskii's, was not alien to his purposes, which had included the enthusiastic promotion of labor history. Although Gorky did place great weight on story and on bringing to life the characters and activities of working-class individuals and of specific groups of workers, the project did not raise very sharply the kind of issues that forced one to take a stand against "lifeless schematicism" and excessive economic determinism. The project allowed Pankratova her continued activity in the labor history field at a time when such history was not being promoted in other Soviet venues. But the onset of the purges, which more or less coincided with Gorky's death in 1936, put an end to this more or less livable interval, confronting her, as we have seen, with another near-death experience.

Her exile period terminated in 1940, Pankratova was fully restored to her post at MGU that year.[60] In an odd way the German attack on the Soviet Union in June 1941 might have come as a relief to her. As a Soviet patriot, which she freely and fiercely declared herself to be, she now had a clear-cut cause, and she worked for it in various capacities throughout the war years, adding to her chronic health problems along the way. Not the least of her tireless wartime efforts on the academic front was her intense participation in the editing and writing of the third and quite tendentious volume of what amounted to an official Soviet history of diplomacy (*Istoriia diplomatii*), edited by Commissar of Enlightenment and Academician Vladimir P. Potemkin and championed by the new and improved academician Tarle.[61] Diplomatic History, hardly a field that had attracted Pankratova greatly in the past, was now seen as a vital part of the international propaganda war. But the war also gave Pankratova a new and very specific cause to champion within the narrower confines of her professional life, one that would repeatedly place her in conflict with many of her colleagues and at times with the highest Party leadership. The war with Germany had almost immediately heightened the already blossoming prewar tendency of many (though by no means all) Soviet historians to enhance the russocentric, nationalist dimension of their interpretations of the past and to defend the scholarship of earlier non-Marxist Russian historians, including aspects of the statist approach. This tendency had been encouraged from above since the mid-1930s, as part of the Stalin-inspired backlash against the Pokrovskii school, now subjected to serious if guarded criticism for its lack of national spirit. But once the war had begun, both historiography and the arts, insofar as they dealt with historical themes (e.g., part 1 of Sergei Eisenstein's film *Ivan Groznyi*, 1944; Aleksei Tolstoi's play *Ivan IV*, 1943; and his novel *Petr I*, 1941-44), were even more prepared, in some important cases quite brazenly, to transform past Russian rulers, statesmen, and military leaders into progressive representatives of Russia's achievements and even harbingers of the accomplishments of the Soviet Union and its supreme leader.[62] In a similar vein, the Empire's annexation of peripheral territories and peoples in centuries gone by, already viewed by Soviet historians as a "lesser evil" (*men'shee zlo*) in relation to Georgia, Ukraine, and a few other areas, was now unabashedly proclaimed by some writers, and more ambiguously by others, to have been a positive good, an accomplishment that was tied to the current defensive war with Germany by Tarle's newly developed notion of space (*prostranstvo*), with Imperial Russia's expansion newly valorized as a precondition for the USSR's ability to withstand the onslaught of Nazi armies.[63]

These tendencies, which were closely paralleled in other academic disciplines,[64] were defended to various degrees by historians Tarle, Iaruzel'skii, and others, and with particular vigor by Professor Aleksei V. Efimov, a Corresponding Member of the Academy of Sciences who, as head of MGU's History Faculty in 1942, was then Pankratova's immediate superior. A specialist in U.S. History and unrestrained commentator on several other fields,[65] Efimov now argued pointedly and openly (and patriotically) that at a time when the very survival of the Soviet Union depended on its alliance with the main bourgeois democracies—the United Kingdom and the United States—it was counterproductive to disparage the Russian past or the scholarly work of Russia's earlier "bourgeois" historians. Similarly, writing in what was almost a "statist" mode, but going even further by suggesting (quite imprudently) that his hero was an enemy of serfdom, the well-known Peter-the-Great specialist Boris Syromiatnikov now staked his reputation on a positive evaluation of Peter's historical role.[66]

After some hesitation, Pankratova chose—and it was clearly her own choice and not the result of Party directives—to take sharp issue with what she portrayed as this "idealization" of the Russian national past at the expense of other "peoples" and with "revisionist" compromises with "bourgeois" historiography.[67] Though never failing to affirm her strong Soviet and even Russian patriotism, and while at first fairly cooperative with some purveyors of the newer "nationalist" tendencies—as witness her participation with Potemkin in the diplomatic history project and her initial willingness to cooperate with Efimov in the production of a volume reevaluating pre-Revolutionary historiography—by the last months of 1942 Pankratova found herself at war with what she now saw as an extreme and dangerous effort to "rehabilitate" the "old bourgeois historians" and resuscitate their methodologies.

On 25 September 1942, Pankratova expressed her concerns in an anxious letter addressed to the then still very influential Georgii F. Aleksandrov, head of the TsK's Agitprop section, candidate member of the TsK, and a frequent if not always consistent defender of the russocentric tendency, and to three other scholars who figured among the most politically powerful members of her profession: Iaroslavskii, Potemkin, and M. V. Mitin. In the letter, Pankratova described her previous day's confrontation with Professor Efimov at a gathering of historians at the Institute of History.[68] Efimov—still her colleague, but now on his way to becoming her archenemy—had sharply criticized an article recently written by Pankratova, prominently placed as the introductory essay in a major "jubilee" collection published by the Academy of Sciences in commemoration of the twenty-fifth anniversary of the October Revolution.[69] Although Pankratova's essay was saturated with expressions of her wartime patriotism and the need for historians to contribute their energies and talents to the "Great Fatherland War," Efimov had charged that Pankratova had presented much too negative a view of Russia's pre-Soviet historians—Kliuchevskii, Miliukov, and others—at a time when Soviet historians should be uniting around the glories of the Russian past and demonstrating to the Soviet Union's newly acquired allies the achievements of past Russian scholarship.

In fact, a careful reading of Pankratova's article reveals that, though unmistakably dismissive of Miliukov, she actually *did* recognize the achievements and talents of some of Russia's leading "bourgeois" historians. She had especially high praise for Sergei Solov'ev, a historian who had played "a great scholarly and socially progressive role" in his times, and who was much superior to his bourgeois contemporaries in Europe; and she even had some positive, respectful, if critical, comments about Kliuchevskii, who, despite his shortcomings, including the inability to develop a single, unified concept of Russia's past, was "a brilliant and talented representative of bourgeois historical science" and who was even worthy of the designation "historian-patriot."[70] Moreover, Pankratova's article included several references to the "heroic traditions of the great Russian people" and the "heroic past of our motherland," and, using the authority of Stalin's famous wartime speech of 7 November 1941 for support, it treated historical figures such as Aleksandr Nevskii, Dmitrii Donskoi, Minin and Pozharskii, and Generals Suvorov and Kutuzov, the precise list of names that had been cited by Stalin, with unconstrained reverence.[71]

To be sure, people wisely hedged their bets, and during the war period, just as it was virtually impossible to find defenders of a more "patriotic" or "russophile" approach who failed to qualify their position with a nod toward class analysis and internationalism, it was very hard to find opponents of excessive Russian nationalism who failed to pay some homage to the Russian past. The difference was one of degree and emphasis, and rival historians were quickly learning how to ferret out the nuances of their opponents' positions when polemics so required. Pankratova's article, for all its gestures in the direction of Russian national pride, did make a point of calling on historians to respect and research the history of the Soviet Union's national minorities, peoples (*narody*), she explained, who were worthy of respectful treatment for their contribution to the war effort.[72] Not quite expressed yet at this point was the additional suggestion that they may have been as worthy of such treatment as the Russians.

Whether as a result of his sensitivity to the language of Pankratova's article or for other objections that emerged from their personal conversations, Efimov was now prepared to denounce Pankratova for her lack of *Russian* national pride. By the same token, in the course of their conflicts, but also on the basis of other recent evidence of his thinking about Russia's past, Pankratova had come to the conclusion that Efimov and certain of his colleagues were moving so far in a russophile direction that they were about to sacrifice their Marxist approach to history on the altar of antifascist solidarity with the bourgeois West. Should this tendency to submit to non-Marxist approaches be allowed to spread to the country's student youth, she insisted in her letter, the results could be disastrous. "I ask you to examine my article," she pleaded defensively with Aleksandrov et al., ". . . an article that summarizes the dogged struggle that has been waged on the historical front for 25 years under the leadership of Lenin and Stalin," and to weigh it against Efimov's "unjust" objections.[73]

Pankratova's appeal to Aleksandrov et al. can easily be read as expressing the typical mindset of a Soviet academic ideologue. The fear that Marxist ideological purity may be sullied, the appeal to higher authority to intervene, the references to Lenin and Stalin all seem to betray the rigidity of a conformist and an unscholarly, uncollegial spirit. But there was more to this appeal, and to the conflict with Efimov, than meets the eye. To begin with, Pankratova knew, she *had* to know, that she was swimming, however cautiously, against the Party stream, in a period when the signals being sent down from above, while sometimes mixed, generally emphasized the need to minimize standard Marxist phraseology, to project flexibility, and to restore national pride. By the same token, though she took a few hard jabs at Pokrovskii in her article[74]—as was by now *de rigueur*—by publicizing even her guarded criticism of Kliuchevskii and others, she was exposing herself to the charge—and it was soon to be heard—of resurrecting Pokrovskii by reopening his old quarrels with his "bourgeois" mentors. Even more to the point, there was real content to some of the complaints that soon evolved from Pankratova's wariness, notions that in part may be defined as a genuine objection to the kind of quasi-chauvinistic, Great Russian history writing that, with Stalin's encouragement, was becoming all too popular in the upper reaches of the profession, at times even anticipating aspects of the postwar anti-cosmopolitan campaign.

As they evolved in the course of the war, Pankratova's more specific fears took two closely related forms: the fear, a reasonable one since Stalin's November 7 speech, that if the claims of pre-Revolutionary Russia's national greatness became excessive, they would be used to justify past conquests and military expansion, turning Russian generals and adventurers not only into acceptable ancestors, but into larger-than-life heroes; and the obverse fear—that the history of the non-Russian nationalities of the Soviet Union would be written in a manner that was disrespectful to their historical movements for independence and their resistance to Russian imperialism. It makes no sense to accuse either Pankratova or her opponents in this debate of being *political*, since as the debate developed over time neither side would doubt the political value and significance of its own position, and the political malevolence of its opponents.

Emotionally, I would like to argue, Pankratova's evolving position, though consistent with her approaches to the Russian past since the time of her apprenticeship with Pokrovskii, derived much of its boldness and energy from a particular source: her personal experiences in Kazakhstan subsequent to her evacuation from Moscow in October 1941 and her extended sojourn thereafter among the intellectual and cultural elite of Alma-Ata, leading to her troubled efforts to publish a multi-authored collection of essays on the history of the Kazakh people(s), *Istoriia Kazakhskoi SSSR*.[75] Although excellent recent studies by David Brandenberger and Peter Blitstein have illuminated what was at stake in the controversy over what was generally thought of as Pankratova's book,[76] it is important to understand the role that was played by personal experience in leading her to her self-appointed position as guardian of the national rights of the Kazakhs, a posture that had little in common with what we know of her earlier worldview but that became increasingly visible in the months that followed her initial clash with Efimov.

The Kazakh story is best told by Pankratova's colleague Nikolai Druzhinin, who followed her from Moscow to Alma-Ata some ten days after her own evacuation, was with her for much of the time she spent there, and collaborated closely with her on the *Istoriia*.[77] According to Druzhinin, soon after the outbreak of war Academician Grekov, then in Moscow serving as Director of the Institute of History, was evacuated to Kazan, leaving Deputy Director Pankratova in charge of the Institute and its *kollektiv* as the German forces bombed and advanced on Moscow. One of her duties was to decide in consultation with the staff which of them would remain in the capital and which would be sent off to a safer haven. On 14 October, with the fate of Moscow still very much in doubt, Pankratova and a large group of the Institute's more senior personnel, like many other Muscovites, departed for Central Asia.

A month later, after extremely difficult journeys, her group and Druzhinin's met up with each other in Alma-Ata. Conditions there were harsh, and the city so terribly overcrowded with evacuees that local officials planned to move them to a smaller, less crowded town. But when Pankratova convinced officials of the Kazakh Commissariat of Enlightenment that her group could be of use to them—by pursuing such activities as holding public lectures for students, soldiers, and others, and preparing a guidebook on how to teach history under wartime conditions —they were permitted to stay. Some twenty of the evacuees (including some family members) were tightly housed at first in one of the rooms of the local Academy of Sciences building, after which, as the Muscovites (along with some evacuated Leningraders) and local scholars became better acquainted, some of the Russian families were invited to move into Kazakh homes while others were placed in the downtown Kazakhstan Hotel. That hotel, which was also the temporary residence of Sergei Eisenstein and other luminaries of the Soviet artistic world, soon became a central locus of intellectual activity and social interaction between Russian and Kazakh scholars. But their lectures also took the itinerant scholar-propagandists away from Alma-Ata for several days and nights at a time, as they moved around the region by bus, car, and even horseback.[78]

Soon Pankratova began to argue for a highly ambitious and unprecedented initiative, first suggested to her by local scholars from the Kazakh Republic's Commissariat of Enlightenment. She proposed to the Kazakh authorities that the combined talents of her group of historians and local scholars be put to use to write a full, collectively-authored history of Kazakhstan, an undertaking still unprecedented in any other Soviet republic, an idea that Kazakh historians had long been considering but felt unable to carry out on their own. An agreement was reached and Pankratova assumed the project's leadership, heading a collective that consisted of a mix of Russian and local scholars. Among the Kazakh, the moving spirit and organizing talent was a brilliant young Moscow-trained historian named Ermukhan Bekmakhanovich Bekmakhanov, then the Kazakh Republic's Deputy Commissar of Enlightenment.[79]

It soon became apparent that one of the themes that *some* of the local historians wished the book to develop as part of the history of the Kazakh people was what was trumpeted as their heroic national resistance to the oppressive colonial policies of the tsarist government. Stressing the Kazakhs' history as fighters was not only flattering to the local population, it was also an obvious way to encourage bold resistance among Kazakhs to the current enemy, the invading German army. The paradox was that, on the one hand, this approach did no more than parallel and echo what Russians were now being told about their *own* heroic feats of the past, while on the other hand it was precisely Russians (among others) that the heroic Kazakhs had been fighting in their own past. This paradox made it rather difficult to promote a crisp and clear-cut "lesser-evil" argument (why should heroic Kazakhs fight Russian expansion if annexation to Russia was a lesser evil, let alone a positive good?), placing Pankratova in a complicated position that was new for her, that of a vigorous advocate of *national* pride, though not, in this case, *Russian* or *Soviet* national pride, but the national pride of one of the Soviet Union's many *narody*.

For practical purposes, among the Russians the day-to-day burden of this difficult task fell less on Pankratova, who at times was dispatched to work in Moscow (where we encountered her, for example, in September 1942) and other venues, than on A. P. Kuchkin, who co-chaired the project in her absence, and, most importantly, Mikhail P. Viatkin, the only genuine specialist on the history of the region among the Russian evacuees (and also a former student of Mikhail Pokrovskii).[80] Within what was to be a multi-authored undertaking, it was Viatkin who was first commissioned to write what proved to be by far the most contentious chapter—the one on the 1837-46 anti-Russian (in the sense of being anti-the-armies-of-the-tsarist-regime) rebellion of Kenesary Kasymov.

The mixed team of Russians and Kazakhs worked steadily on the research and writing for the better part of a year, which is not to say that the work went smoothly. Aside from the burdensome material conditions, there were serious and at times stormy ideological conflicts within the group, interpretive differences that did not always line the combatants up in neat formation as Russians versus Kazakhs. The most significant fight was over Mikhail Viatkin's draft chapter, since Viatkin insisted on representing Kasymov's armed struggle against the government of Nicholas I, a topic he knew very well and had written about in the past, as admirable and heroic: a colonized people was resisting conquest by the "gendarme of Europe" and fighting against incorporation in the tsarist "prison of peoples." The controversial Viatkin was eventually replaced by Bekmakhanov, but the controversy remained the same, for Bekmakhanov's more restrained representation of Kasymov was not restrained enough for the opponents of alleged Kazakh nationalism. Though no member of the team seems to have categorically denied that the Kazakhs' incorporation into the Russian Empire was in some sense positive ("progressive"), at least in the long run (would the Kazakhs have been better off under the "feudal despotisms" of Khiva, Kokand, or Bukhara? Or under China?), some participants, including even some Kazakh scholars, were wary of any hint of praise of Kazakh resistance to Russia. Viewing these events from what might be called a more Muscovite perspective, they valorized the very territorial expansion of Russia that Kasymov had opposed, an expansion that made possible the current boundaries of the Soviet state, the very "space" that was being defended against German aggression.[81]

As leader of the group it was Pankratova's obligation to resolve such disagreements. However, by the fall of 1942, during the final editing process, the conflicts had become so bitter that Academician Grekov himself, Director of the Institute of History, had to be summoned to Alma-Ata from Tashkent, now the evacuation center for most members of the Institute, to soothe and reconcile the contending parties. The book, including Bekmakhanov's controversial chapter, was then revised and completed under Pankratova's guidance and published in the early summer of 1943, when Pankratova, Druzhinin, and their colleagues ended their sojourns in Central Asia and returned definitively to Moscow. Pankratova left Alma-Ata a highly esteemed and even beloved figure. Her hosts awarded her with the title *zasluzhennyi deiatel' nauki Kazakhskoi SSR*.[w] To honor Pankratova for her work on the *Istoriia* and her other services to Kazakhstan before her departure, local dignitaries had even organized a special banquet, where speakers uttered "many warm words of gratitude" to her and to her group.[82]

Unfortunately for Pankratova, her book's reception in Moscow was much more mixed than it was in Alma-Ata, especially at the upper echelons of the academic-political hierarchy. With the strong backing of Georgii Aleksandrov and his associates at Agitprop, where russocentrism and, in the words of Peter Blitstein, "impatience with non-Russian efforts to develop their own 'heroic traditions'" had been growing apace,[83] critics of the book, and the Kasymov chapter in particular, wasted little time in attacking it for its alleged ratification of Kazakh nationalism, for its lack of a fully "class" perspective on the Kazakh national past (including its failure to grasp that rebels like Kasymov represented the interests of the Kazakh ruling class and British imperialists), and, most pointedly, for its "anti-Russian" bias. Being accused of insufficient attention to class analysis was an unusual position for Pankratova, the former student of Pokrovskii and devotee of Marxist approaches (although it is true that Pokrovskii, while not encouraging ethno-centered research, would have had no problem in principle with the defense of the struggle of an "imprisoned" people,[84] which is the way he had interpreted the now equally controversial rebellion of Shamil'). Nevertheless, still holding the eminent position of Deputy Director of the Institute of History, and armed with the allusions in the 1934 Stalin-Zhdanov-Kirov *Zamechaniia* to Lenin's description of Imperial Russia as the "prison of peoples," Pankratova appeared to occupy a strong

---

w. "Distinguished Scientist of the Kazakh SSR."

position from which to defend herself and her collaborators.

In so doing, however, it was almost inevitable that she would link her defense of the *Istoriia*, and especially of Kazakh national feeling, to the issues she had raised in her earlier letter to Aleksandrov, specifically to her accusation that Efimov and others were resurrecting bourgeois historiography and, with it, ethnic Russian nationalism and even chauvinism. The linkage, though questionable as formulated, was not exactly far-fetched, especially at a time when scholars like Tarle, fired up with genuine wartime patriotism following Germany's attack on the Soviet Union, were making increasingly positive pronouncements, with strong nationalist intonation, about the value of Imperial Russia's territorial expansion.[85]

Matters reached a head at the end of 1943, when the *Istoriia*, having been nominated for the Stalin Prize, and after a positive initial reception by the prize committee, was termed "anti-Russian" and was torn to shreds by the historian Aleksei Ivanovich Iakovlev (like Pankratova, a corresponding member of the Academy of Sciences) for, among other things, its failure to grasp the necessity of Russia's expansion to secure borders.[86] Under the influence of Iakovlev's scathing review, the prize committee soon reversed its position and the nomination was withdrawn. Shortly thereafter, an angry Pankratova was moved to turn to no less a figure than Andrei Zhdanov (then located in Leningrad) to express her dismay, which she did at great length and with great passion.[87] Her letter raised all of the worries we have seen her belaboring since 1942, though now in bolder language—excessive Russian patriotism, the glorification of past Russian military conquests and conquerors, and the reevaluation of pre-Soviet historians, especially Kliuchevskii and his "school," all of this summed up by Pankratova as the "rejection of Marxism-Leninism." She even managed to add some new concerns, such as the rehabilitation of idealism and Panslavism. But it is important to emphasize that her (not necessarily Marxist) good feelings about the Kazakhs constituted a central part of her plea. To be sure, Pankratova saved this note for the last part of her letter, though I read this as a sign of its importance, a saving of the most powerful blow for last. "Is it right," she asked with lots of visible emotion and little discernible Marxism, "to deprive the peoples [*narody*] of the USSR of their heroic past and their national heroes simply because they fought against the national and colonial yoke of tsarism?" Linking this rhetorical question with her own experience among the Kazakhs and other nationalities, she continued:

I am particularly upset [*Menia osobenno volnuet*] by this last tendency, which is likely to have enormous consequences of the most negative character among the peoples of our motherland. At the present time in all the Soviet republics' books are being energetically written dedicated to the history of the individual nations. Interest in their own national histories, in the heroic past of their own people, in their fighters for freedom and independence has grown to an exceptional extent. [*Istorik*, p. 226.]

Then, turning specifically to her Kazakhs, Pankratova described the wonderful reception *Istoriia* had received by both Kazakh and Russian historians and the enthusiastic letters about the book sent to her by Kazakh soldiers fighting *for the USSR* at the front. It was a book, she asserted, that "teaches the friendship of peoples" and instills non-Russians with "respect and love for the great Russian people." Yet not only had the book been denounced in a major statement by Iakovlev to the Stalin Prize committee, his position had since been given a "sympathetic reception" by "Comrade Aleksandrov," the same influential Agitprop director with whom she already was in conflict over "bourgeois tendencies" in Soviet scholarship. Aleksandrov, she complained, even went so far as to denounce the book for being "anti-Russian" and for neglecting to show that without annexation by Russia, the Kazakhs would have remained a "people without history" (an indirect reference to Hegel that may have accounted for Pankratova's thrust against idealism, though she had to have known that Engels used the same language in 1848). Of course, Pankratova insisted, the authors of *Istoriia* "could not have interpreted the Kazakh people as a people without history," for the Kazakhs were a people with "a very rich history," as the highly qualified contributors to the volume had clearly demonstrated. As to the charge that the book was anti-Russian, one merely had to read it dispassionately to see that "from the first to the last page it was penetrated with a striving to show the deep historical tie between the Russian and Kazakh peoples" and the Kazakhs' common struggle with "progressive" Russians against tsarism. But what her detractors were demanding, she suggested, was the inclusion in the volume of a misleading portrait of "tsarist colonizers as the bearers of progress and freedom." Had that been the case, she asked, why, then, did we need the October Revolution to liberate Russia's oppressed peoples?

To justify her decision to appeal to the chief Communist of Leningrad for assistance, Pankratova, writing again with unrestrained sentiment, invoked the widespread concept of *shefstvo*,[x] pointing to that city's role as Kazakhstan's past and present "patron" (*shef*)—in effect, its sister (or big-brother) city:

> Both in the past and at present Leningraders have provided Kazakhstan with invaluable assistance in all areas of its life and culture. In Kazakhstan I have seen and felt with what limitless love the Kazakhs speak of Leningraders as their good-friends and blood-brothers. . . . For them your word, just like the word of their deceased friend Comrade Kirov, is law.

Her plea was that Zhdanov read the book, evaluate it, summon her to Leningrad to discuss it, and—though this was not said in so many words—overrule Aleksandrov and reverse the decision to deny the book the Stalin Prize (a reversal that would of course have required the approval of Stalin himself). Whatever the shortcomings of the book, she concluded, it was wrong to "take away their heroic fighting traditions from the Kazakh people and declare it a people without history."[88]

When two months had passed without a reply to her letter, Pankratova tried again. Seemingly at a loss for what to do next, she explained to Zhdanov that she had even considered a direct appeal to Stalin, but she dropped the idea, "clearly recognizing that at a time of war we dare not take away even one of his valuable minutes." Her immediate goal was to gain a personal interview with Zhdanov (who had more than his share of war-related problems to attend to in Leningrad), if for no other purpose than to learn where he stood and have him provide her with proper "orientation." Pankratova pleaded with him: she had gone far out on a limb; her situation vis-à-vis her superiors was by now desperate; and she no longer knew what to say to her colleagues and students and to political propagandists. She was finding it impossible to work until it was all clarified. Besides, she confessed to Zhdanov, she had "no one else to turn to."[89]

Two weeks later, having still received no response, Pankratova made the ultimate move: she directed her complaints to the TsK itself. In a long

---

x. guidance, sponsorship.

letter addressed to Stalin, Zhdanov, Georgii Malenkov, and Shcherbakov, this time writing in a much more sober and official-sounding style, she laid out her entire case in great detail.[90] She began with a direct criticism of Agitprop for its failure to critique or adopt the Institute of History's special plan for historians' activity under wartime conditions, thereby leaving the entire profession at sea with regard to what was required of it and which positions were or were not acceptable to the Party. This lack of clarity, she argued, had opened the door to certain historians, especially those of the "old school," to question and revise Marxist-Leninist positions in historical scholarship (NB: no mention of Stalinist positions!). For this, paradoxically, she blamed her enemy Efimov (hardly a representative of the "old school"), while praising a true member of the old school (if such there still was), the sixteenth-century specialist Sergei V. Bakhrushin, her former colleague at MGU (arrested in 1930 but soon rehabilitated), the person who had first brought Efimov's misconduct to her attention.

Pankratova's list of Efimov's transgressions basically repeated her earlier charges: he had called for an excessively sympathetic approach to the Kliuchevskiis and the Miliukovs, had argued that Soviet historians were their legitimate intellectual heirs, and maintained that the wartime alliance with England and the United States required a more positive approach to bourgeois historiography and less of an emphasis on class struggle. Since Pankratova's defense of class analysis would have made it easier for her adversaries to link her with Pokrovskii, however, she now cleverly covered her flank by making it a point to attack her erstwhile mentor's supposed dictum (by now a ubiquitous attack-shibboleth), that history was politics projected back on the past, by accusing Efimov of practicing precisely that kind of history. In so doing, she argued, he had somehow given a green light to Syromiatnikov's un-Marxist representations of Peter the Great as well as to Eisenstein's misleading representation of Ivan the Terrible. To transform such rulers as well as several Russian generals into heroic national figures was a "modernizing" of Russian history, thereby blurring the boundary between tsarist Russia and the Soviet Union and muddying the minds of Soviet youth.[91] Pankratova had to be aware that such accusations, perhaps the criticisms of Eisenstein's *Ivan* most of all, risked placing her at odds with Stalin himself.

As in her previous letter to Zhdanov, these and other accusations culminated in her complaint about the development that disturbed her the most: the dual tendency to cheer retroactively for the conquest of Russia's borderlands and to devalue the resistance to those conquests by peoples like her friends the Kazakhs. Placing part of the blame for the current situation on Academician Tarle, who had questioned the concept of "the prison of peoples," Pankratova retold the story of Iakovlev's hatchet job on the *Istoriia Kazakhskoi SSSR* and the support he had received from Aleksandrov, Potemkin, and other influential figures. Blithely contradicting her own denial that history was politics projected on the past, Pankratova defended her book by reminding the TsK that it was written "at a very difficult time [*tiazheloe vremia*], 1941-42, with the goal of showing the Kazakhs that they needed to defend the achievements of the October socialist revolution, which had guaranteed them genuine freedom, independence and a civilized [*kul'turnaia*], happy life." The attacks on the book now threatened to counteract this positive effect, for if the Kazakhs are told that "their fighting traditions, their leaders, and their uprisings against tsarism were reactionary and counter to the interests of the Russian people, this will do unavoidable and, more to the point, unnecessary and harmful damage to their national feeling." Pankratova conceded (was she thinking of the Chechens?) that there were a few peoples whose conduct in the course of the present war was less than patriotic, but not the Kazakh people, who, "as far as we know, has proven itself quite well [*neplokho proiavil sebia*] on the front," producing close to a hundred official Heroes of the Soviet Union.[92]

Concluding with yet another plea, Pankratova, speaking in the name of her collaborators on *Istoriia*, ended her letter with a request that the TsK organize a serious discussion with the authors of the book, one that would in the end produce a "correct line" on the questions of principle raised by the book, correcting its shortcomings where needed. Of course she was asking for a correct line not simply on the question of Kazakh resistance, but on the broader issue of interpreting Russia's imperial(ist) past.

Almost certainly as a direct response to Pankratova's appeal, the TsK decided to organize a special conference in Moscow, consisting of most of the Soviet Union's leading historians and some high-ranking TsK members, to debate and decide the issues that had been raised. Anticipating this portentous event and fearing, perhaps, that Pankratova would be able to make a convincing case in the course of the debate, Aleksandrov decided on a preemptive strike: mobilizing his own Deputy Director of Agitprop, P. N. Fedoseev, and the editor of the Party newspaper *Pravda*, P. N. Pospelov, he composed with their assistance a powerful and comprehensive memorandum sharply criticizing the current character of the Soviet Union's historical profession, with Pankratova clearly placed in the cross-hairs as his central target; the memorandum was addressed to the leading Secretaries of the TsK—Malenkov, Shcherbatov, and A. A. Andreev, precisely the men in charge of the forthcoming conference.[93]

Although the memorandum managed to accuse Pankratova of every conceivable scholarly and political sin, even lumping her together with her adversary Iakovlev as partisans of "German idealism," the centerpiece of its attack on her was the supposed anti-Russianism of her *Istoriia Kazakhskoi SSR*, to which Aleksandrov devoted an entire section entitled "The Anti-Leninist Views of Certain Historians Regarding the National Question."[94] Following the convention of citing Lenin and Stalin as the main authors whom the culprit dared to contradict, Aleksandrov was in fact much more attuned to Pankratova's slights against Russia, her "idealization" of the Kazakh past (p. 199), and her failure to present the annexation of Kazakh areas as a lesser evil (comparable to the TsK's position on the annexations of Georgia and Poland, which Pankratova *had* endorsed), than to her alleged violations of Marxist-Leninist-Stalinist orthodoxy. Russia, he complained, is depicted in *Istoriia* as "the most evil and most dangerous enemy of the non-Russian peoples, and the annexation of these peoples to Russia is viewed as an absolute evil for them." Moreover, *Istoriia* had failed to demonstrate "the leading role of the Russian people in the formation and development of a multinational state in Russia" (p. 197).

These serious errors, which played into the hands of Kazakh (and Bashkir) anti-Soviet "bourgeois nationalists" (p. 200), were linked by Aleksandrov to the equally grave fault of (allegedly) claiming that the Russian people were culturally backward relative to the rest of Europe, a sin for which both Pankratova and her close ally Militsa Nechkina were also taken to task, mainly on the basis of the textbooks they had edited before the war. Then, to further bolster his case against Pankratova, Aleksandrov raised the ghost of her controversial essay in Viatkin's 1942 collection, *Sovetskaia istoricheskaia nauka za 25 let*,[y] adding to Efimov's questionable charge that she had slandered Russia's bourgeois historians the further accusations that she failed to cite an important 1941 article by Stalin and, more generally, that she had demonstrated how closely linked she still remained to her by now long-departed mentor, now truly a ghost,

---

y. *Soviet Historical Science over the Last Twenty-Five Years.*

Pokrovskii. On the basis of all this and other similar "evidence," Aleksandrov concluded that Pankratova, along with Nechkina, Bakhrushin, and several of Pankratova's other colleagues had conducted themselves in a manner that failed to promote "the national pride of the Soviet people" and "love of the historical past of our motherland" (p. 197).

Oddly, if not incomprehensibly, the same memorandum that focused so sharply on the evils of anti-Russian sentiment contained an addendum on the "Great-Power nationalist errors" of some Russian historians (pp. 201 -204), errors, however, that for the most part, claimed the memorandum, were not to be found in print but in unpublished manuscripts and oral reports (p. 201). Here the villains were not Pankratova, Nechkina, and their cohort, but some of their primary antagonists, including Iakovlev and Tarle himself. What was odd in this case was that Aleksandrov, without acknowledging it, was echoing the very charges that the villain of his piece, Pankratova, had been leveling against the very same historians, including the charge of belittling the aspirations of the country's non-Russian nation-alities (Iakovlev) and failure to acknowledge that the Russian Empire had been the "gendarme of Europe" (Tarle). Of course these errors, which brought to mind the historiographical writings of Kadets and Mensheviks, were violations of *leninsko-stalinskaia politika*[z] as well (pp. 202, 204).

The first meeting, opened by TsK Secretary Malenkov, was held on 29 May, some seventeen days after Pankratova sent her letter. The full conference consisted of five long and lively sessions, the last one taking place on 8 July.[95] The Party leadership, Stalin included, had to have seen these historiographical controversies as bearing enormous political import for men such as TsK Secretaries Shcherbakov (who presided at all the sessions), Malenkov, and Andreev to have participated at a time when the Soviet army was preparing its major offensive on the Belorussian front.[96]

Pankratova played a very active part at the sessions, vigorously defending her positions and her *Istoriia Kazakhskoi SSR* (again described by some speakers as "anti-Russian") in the course of an often acrimonious and heated debate that drove her to the point of "moral and physical exhaustion."[97] She was supported by Militsa Nechkina (very effectively, in Pankratova's opinion), Nikolai Druzhinin, Arkadii Sidorov (who challenged the more extreme versions of the lesser-evil thesis), and several of their closest associates, though some of Pankratova's erstwhile colleagues and

z. Leninist-Stalinist policy.

collaborators, most notably the *ikapist* Isaak Mints, then dean of MGU's History Faculty, disappointed her by taking what she saw as soft and middling positions. She was opposed by Iakovlev, Efimov, and others, including, at the last two sessions, Tarle, who was hastily summoned from Georgia via a telegram from Aleksandrov. Tarle by now had come to represent the very antithesis of Pankratova's views on the presentation of Russia's national history. Reflecting, no doubt, his bitter memory of their past conflicts in the Akademicheskoe delo as well as his anger at Pankratova's more recent attacks, he at one point nastily called Pankratova and her supporters "fledglings from Pokrovskii's nest." Pankratova, in turn, who considered Tarle the unofficial leader and inspiration of the opposing group, described him in equally unflattering terms, privately telling her friends that, compared to Tarle, Pokrovskii was an "innocent baby" (*nevinnyi mladenets*).[98]

While their efforts at the conference did bear some fruit, to a great extent Pankratova and her allies had argued in vain. Some significant compromises were allowed and the attacks on *Istoriia* were soon toned down, but Pankratova's positions came in for some very rough criticism both at the conference and subsequently, and it is highly unlikely this would have been allowed had most of the TsK, including Zhdanov, and probably Stalin himself, not rejected important parts of her argument.[99]

The practical outcome was a mandatory rewriting of the *Istoriia* for its second edition (not published until 1949), in which some though not all of the book's original statements of admiration for Kazakh resistance movements were expunged or modified. Aleksandrov (whose own fortunes were to take a bad turn after the war) played a major role in producing this outcome, as indicated by a memorandum he addressed to Zhdanov, Malenkov, and Shcherbakov in which he condemned Pankratova for her "anti-Party behavior" and tendentiousness, for going over the head of her local Party organizations by reporting on the conference proceedings, and on the related correspondence in her letters to her friends, for her alleged claim to be Russia's only truly orthodox Marxist historian, for her pernicious influence on the Kazakh historians, and for a host of other unforgivable sins, including her past career as a Left SR and—a brand-new charge—her participation in a Trotskyite group.[100]

Ignored by the TsK (except, at long last, by Zhdanov), Pankratova had little choice but to accept the limitations of what at best were her few small victories and abandon her struggle for full vindication. In effect, she capitulated to the Communist leaders whose *ultimate* authority she had never questioned in principle, though her capitulation involved no *public* humiliation and her language of submission, contained in a letter dated 7 September and addressed to Zhdanov, was carefully crafted so as to avoid any clear declaration that she had been wrong on the substantive issues. As Blitstein indicates, Zhdanov, while rejecting most of Pankratova's views, was also quite critical of her adversaries, including Tarle and Iakovlev,[101] and it is likely that he adopted a similar posture at the private meeting that he held with Pankratova prior to September 7, where he encouraged her to recant and suggested that she write such a letter. As a consequence, she wrote to Zhdanov:

> I am sending my declaration to you in accordance with your proposal. My only request to you is that you believe me when I tell you I have deeply acknowledged and am suffering greatly from my error and my guilt. This is all the more difficult for me in that *I was always convinced that I was fighting for the Party line in the field of history.* I will never forget the lesson that you taught me during our discussion. Help me.[102]

Lacking Zhdanov's protection, some of Pankratova's closest Kazakh collaborators, most notably Bekmakhanov, were destined to suffer much more from this affair than Pankratova.[103]

Pankratova truly had nine lives. Having capitulated to authority, in the wake of the victorious Fatherland War she was once again forgiven and even rewarded with honors. Denied the Stalin prize for *Istoriia Kazanskoi SSSR*, she received it instead for her defense of recent Soviet foreign policy in the edited volume, *Istoriia diplomatii*. Despite her controversial past, she retained both her Party membership and her position as corresponding member of the Academy, and, of course, her other teaching and research positions in Moscow. Yet Pankratova was barely done licking the wounds from her wartime troubles when she was confronted with a new challenge, launched by the early signals of what would become the "anti-cosmopolitan campaign," itself—apart from its anti-Semitism—a continuation of the wartime valorization of Russian national pride, but with an added virulence and viciousness provided by the burgeoning atmosphere of the Cold War.[104] One of the campaign's early historian-victims was the very serious Leningrad historian of Russian labor and early Russian Marxism, Esfir' Abramovna Korol'chuk, then a teacher at the Herzen Pedagogical Institute, research scholar (*nauchnyi sotrudnik*) at the Leningrad Istpart,[aa] and a specialist since the 1920s on the political activities and ideology of Petersburg workers in the 1870s and beyond.[105] In 1946, the very year of Andrei Zhdanov's still rather vague report that to some extent prefigured the full-blown attack on "rootless cosmopolitanism" that was to follow, Korol'chuk published a valuable and, for the times, rather balanced and at first well-received monograph on the Northern Union of Russian Workers (1878-80).[106] By 1949, however, against the background of the more sharply drawn and ideologically driven campaign of 1947-48, launched by Zhdanov (ironically) in the course of his assault on Georgii Aleksandrov's history of Western philosophy,[107] Korol'chuk and her by then three-year-old book were subjected to scathing attacks at a special meeting of members of the Leningrad Istpart, then headed by S. P. Kniazev (also a nemesis of Pankratova's during the conflicts of 1953-56, described below). The assault was led by E. A. Sokolova, a graduate of the IKP, who, among other far-fetched charges, took her colleague to task for underestimating the international significance of Russia's early labor movement, overstating the relative importance of West European labor movements, and exaggerating the Northern Union's links to the Populist intelligentsiia, a group of charges that were then summed up as "cosmopolitanism."[108] As a result of the denunciations, and with the collaboration of Kniazev, Korol'chuk was removed from her position at the Herzen Institute and denied academic employment anywhere in Leningrad; her book was banned and somewhat later she was expelled from the Party. There were also efforts to deprive her of her recently awarded Doctor's degree from the Institute of History, where she had submitted "*Severnyi Soiuz*" as her dissertation. These actions were clearly intended as a battle in the anti-cosmopolitan campaign, and for supporters of Korol'chuk and admirers of her book to rise to her defense must be seen as an act of daring, especially for a supporter with a past history of "near misses." Pankratova, whose still undisputed prominence in the labor history field and corresponding membership in the Academy of Sciences would have made any criticism of Korol'chuk a lethal blow, instead assigned herself a leadership role among Korol'chuk's defenders. Though their personal relationship probably dated to the mid-

---

aa. Institute of Party History.

1930s, when Korol'chuk too was involved in the *Istoriia fabrik* project, Pankratova embraced the work of Korol'chuk on its merits and now chose to act as her premier advocate. Working in close collaboration with three other prominent historians, Druzhinin, Nechkina, and Aleksei Sidorov—all of them her allies in the battles at the 1944 historians' conference—Pankratova addressed a lengthy, closely argued petition in Korol'chuk's behalf to V. M. Andrianov, first secretary of the Leningrad obkom and gorkom, with copies to Iurii Zhdanov, the deceased Andrei's politically influential son, and the historian P. N. Pospelov, both important members of the TsK.[109]

Both a defense of Korol'chuk and a scathing counterattack on her detractors, especially Sokolova, the letter began with the statement that the authors considered it their "social duty" (*obshchestvennyi dolg*) to call attention to the "scandalous business" (*vopiiushchee delo*) of Korol'chuk's "scholarly and political discrediting." Pankratova and her colleagues astutely turned the tables on Korol'chuk's critics by correctly stating that Lenin's claim that Russian workers were the world's most politically advanced and revolutionary, used as an argument by Sokolova, was meant to apply only to the turn of the century, and not to the 1870s. This mode of argument—quotation versus counter-quotation, accusations of "falsification," and so on—was of course too deeply ingrained by now in Soviet academic discourse to be avoidable; whichever side of a polemical confrontation one was on, the other side had to be represented as at worst a betrayer of the country and the people, at best a distorter of the views of Lenin and Stalin and a falsifier. (The letter even manages to cite Stalin's *Short Course* as an authority on the subject at hand!) Nevertheless, the letter argued Korol'chuk's case at length and in detail, and scored several important and accurate points, including the point that Sokolova's claim that Korol'chuk had exaggerated the influence of populism on the Northern Union was a distortion if not a complete reversal of Korol'chuk's argument (though Korol'chuk may have hurt herself in the eyes of her detractors simply by treating the Populists with any degree of respect). The tone of the petition was by no means fawning. Its strongly worded request for an end to the "baseless campaign against Korol'chuk" was cast in language that reflected the self-confidence and academic status of the authors. Moreover, the petition resulted in a partial victory in that Korol'chuk not only avoided arrest, but was also reinstated in the Party and permitted to remain in Leningrad. But her career was seriously damaged, and Pankratova, who continued to consult with Korol'chuk about her own research, felt obliged to devote considerable energy to assisting her, morally, professionally, and financially, and helping her, albeit unsuccessfully, to obtain new academic employment. Though Korol'chuk was ultimately able to resume her studies, as late as 1956 Pankratova was still complaining of the obstacles placed before her colleague's efforts to find academic work and publish her research.[110]

In 1949 Pankratova was appointed to the editorial board of the Institute of History's recently founded journal, *Voprosy istorii* (hereafter *VI*). For her first few years on the board, which coincided with the anti-cosmopolitan campaign, the only visible evidence, apart from her support of Korol'chuk, that suggested nonconformist behavior was her still energetic though behind-the-scenes defense (together with Nechkina, at first) of historians, specifically G. Guseinov, who had "too" positive a take on "progressive" national uprisings against the tsarist régime, especially that of Shamil'.[111] Her overall tendency, perhaps an expression of her chastening, was to put aside her wartime fears of Russian nationalist trends in her profession, as witness the hard line she took in 1949, sounding much like a moderate anti-cosmopolitan, against "objectivist" historians who, as she put it, displayed "bourgeois" tendencies that denied the positive features of Russia's past by professing the "non-independence of the political and cultural development of our country."[112] She seems to have resigned herself to the standards of Suslov's dictums in general, even while rising to the defense of particular individuals, a pattern that remained in place until Stalin's death on 4 March 1953 and the ensuing first signs of the "thaw."

Khrushchev's ascendancy after Stalin's death roughly coincided with Pankratova's highest elevation within the Soviet academic hierarchy. That fall she was granted the *Orden Lenina*[bb] for her thirty years of "irreproachable" (*bezuprechnaia*) service and was finally made a full member of the Academy—honors, as she told one of her most intimate friends, that filled her with great joy.[113] In 1954 she was elected (or "selected," as we might now say) to the Supreme Soviet of the USSR. Much more important for our immediate purposes was her promotion to the post of *VI*'s editor-in-chief, marking the beginning of the final, highly controversial phase of her troubled career. The story of the rise and fall of *VI*'s liberal, antidogmatic, revisionist spirit from 1953 to 1957 has been told and told very well by several historians,[114] and need not be repeated here except in

---

bb. Order of Lenin.

broadest outline. In the earlier accounts of that episode, however, it was Eduard Burdzhalov—Nekrich has dubbed him "the motor" of the journal's revisionist period, and others have dubbed the entire episode "the Burdzhalov Affair"[115]—who received the lion's share of scholarly attention, in part because his role was indeed impressive, even heroic, and in part because he himself wrote some of the most daring revisionist pieces, especially his controversial 1956 articles on the hot topic of the Bolsheviks' (especially Stalin's) attitudes toward the Provisional Government in March and April 1917, prior to Lenin's decisive role after arriving in Petrograd in April.[116] My sole purpose here is to highlight the neglected role of Pankratova and to reconstruct the story of this the last major episode of her strife-filled life.[117,cc]

First a very brief summary to refresh memories: One could think of the start of the *VI* story as the upsurge in Stalin's public interest in scholarly issues that was marked by his 1950 attack on the theories of Nikolai Marr in *Pravda*.[118] This was the first of a number of Stalin's new forays into (pseudo-) scholarship in linguistics, economics, and other areas that continued up to the XIXth Party Congress in 1952.[119] By then Stalin was too feeble to assert himself with energy, but the focus on scholarship at the Congress included some harsh criticism of the Institute of History and its undertakings, including *VI*, which was also criticized at the time in the pages of the Party organ *Kommunist*. Over the preceding few years, the journal's editorial board had been dominated by people appointed in and around 1949, and the membership reflected the ethos of the anti-cosmopolitan campaign. Its articles, as Kan recalls, were considered unsatisfactory both by Stalinist apparatchiki and serious historians, albeit for different reasons.[120]

After Stalin's death, the new Party leadership, acting mainly through the Institute, called for the reorganization of *VI*'s editorial board, with the aim of raising the level of that journal's articles, many of which had been little more than an echo chamber for Stalin's *Short Course* and his subsequent "scholarly" pronouncements. The editorial board was reshuffled. Some, but not all time-serving hacks were removed and, more importantly, new blood was added to the board in the person of younger, more energetic and more professional historians, among them veterans of the recent war. Pankratova was promoted to the top position, while Burdzhalov was named as her deputy, both with the approval of top TsK Secretaries

---

cc. Author's note in the text: [NB: *Final version will go beyond this limited purpose and provide a closer, fresh analysis of some of issues at stake on the basis of new materials.*].

Suslov and Pospelov. They in turn were authorized to reconstitute the full editorial board, after which the board received the personal approval of Khrushchev himself.

In the course of the next three years the journal began to publish both lead editorials and solid research papers that in many respects challenged the Stalinist orthodoxies of the past, often taking on the sacred cows of Soviet historiography while seeking safety under the protective mantle of Lenin. A wide range of topics, both substantive and theoretical, were now subjected to fresh treatment. The topics included the nature of Russian serfdom, pre-Revolutionary controversies over feudalism, Imperial Russia's relative "backwardness," Western influences on Russian history, Russia's alleged priority in scientific discovery and technological invention, the (re)evaluation of Shamil' (once again!), Plekhanov's role in the revolutionary movement, the origins of Lenin's notion of a worker-peasant revolutionary alliance (whether he already anticipated this idea in the 1890s or only in the wake of 1905), the revolutionary dedication of the Menshevik and SR parties (especially in 1905), the nature of the February Revolution (Burdzhalov's specialty), conflicts between Lenin and Stalin in 1917 (addressed by Burdzhalov, though not until 1956), spontaneity versus the "laws of history" under capitalism, the relation between the October Revolution and the subsequent civil war, American intervention in that war, and, a topic that received inordinate amounts of attention in part because of its implications for the interpretation of the historical role of Stalin, the proper periodization of Soviet history and the need to distinguish between the history of Soviet society and the history of the ruling Communist Party. In addition, there were numerous important initiatives in various areas of non-Russian/non-Soviet history (*vseobshchaia istoriia*), including the United States, and the pages of the journal were increasingly open to the writings of Western historians, or at least the "progressive" ones.

Just how daring these new approaches were obviously depends on one's standard of comparison. Viewed from a distance and against the background of a wide range of historiographical possibilities, it is easy to see many of the attempted "Leninist revisions" of these years as modest in scope and overly cautious. This is especially the case if one focuses on two limitations that even the most daring authors set for themselves (or that were set for them): (1) First, although "citationism" was widely condemned by the new editors, citing Lenin's many words of wisdom, useful as they were if only by dint of their promiscuity, remained a ubiquitous practice, as did the practice of criticizing the position of others as failing to conform to genuine Marxism-Leninism (though no longer Stalinism); (2) and second, though following Khrushchev's lead, *VI* historians were prepared to attack the "cult of personality" as part of the reinterpretation process (as were many of their opponents, albeit in more guarded fashion), they, like Khrushchev, were reluctant to go as far as to attack *Stalin* directly (let alone to wrestle seriously with the issue of Stalin*ism*) or to raise the question of the Party's own role in permitting the cult to arise and persist. Both kinds of inhibition reflected the need of the revisionists to display themselves as historians who still wrote under the banner of Soviet patriotism (a large enough banner, to be sure), especially as they began to come under fire from high Party authorities. But at the same time, viewed up close, as it were, from inside the admittedly small public sphere that was just beginning to be permitted within a still quite totalitarian framework, these revisions had some powerful components. They not only threatened certain well-established orthodoxies, something that had been done before, as we saw, in times of flux, but they also began in practice to question the very concept of a historical scholarship driven by central directives, a scholarship in which disagreements were dismissed as deviations and deviators were dismissed as enemies of the people.

It is against this background that we need to evaluate Pankratova's role. She had certainly not been chosen as editor-in-chief in anticipation of very radical new departures. Despite her by now numerous engagements in controversy, she had, after all, always managed to come back to the Party line and to accept Party discipline. Like Burdzhalov, she was a Communist whose Party membership dated back to the Civil War. Unlike Burdzhalov (a russified Armenian from Baku), she was a "genuine" *Russian*, and one with a genuine record of "Soviet patriotism" and wartime activism. At the same time, she had an excellent scholarly reputation, had steered clear of any extreme positions in the anti-cosmopolitan campaign, and, while her recent writings were not devoid of routine praise of Stalin, her language had been relatively subdued in this regard.[dd] In short, she seemed like just the right, moderate, responsible person to introduce serious improvements in the quality of *VI* without moving forward in too radically revisionist a direction.

---

dd. Author's note in the text: [add a few examples here from her three Intros to *Rabochee dvizhenie v Rossii v XIX veke*].

Although often opposed by some editorial board members, Pankratova managed quite quickly to take the reins of the board, in part by making personnel changes in the important administrative and research staff (the *sotrudniki*) that guaranteed its reliability in carrying out her wishes. In addition to many of the younger members, she also had the strong support on the board of major figures like her close friend Druzhinin, with whom she had been through thick and thin during the war and longer. During the first year or year and a half of the new *VI* regime, the *spokoinyi period*,[ee] as Kan has called it,[121] what Pankratova introduced was not so much fresh historical writing as a fresh spirit of collegial interaction, one in which she insisted on an end to personal recriminations, personal accusations, vulgarization, oversimplification, and argument by "citation," and a new emphasis on open and collegial debate, access to and use of archives, and, not to be forgotten, respect for the work of foreign historians. In some ways this was as harsh a rebuke of the spirit of Stalinism as could be made, though it was still too early to label it as such, and from time to time Stalin was still cited in the journal as a scholarly authority, especially in the new board's first few issues (fall 1953) and even, though very rarely, in 1954

Other changes for which Pankratova personally pressed the TsK Secretariat with considerable if not complete success included: a larger staff, higher salaries and academic status for the *sotrudniki* (her own salary and Burdzhalov's were quite high), more spacious office accommodations, a better quality of paper, and the right to pay honoraria to Westerners, whose contributions she wished to encourage, in *valiuta*.[ff] The size of the journal (number of print sheets) was also increased. As a result of some of these improvements, the circulation of the journal began to increase steadily and then dramatically. Clearly there was a demand in the Soviet Union for a better kind of history writing and in a more attractive journal. In keeping with her past performance, Pankratova also made a serious effort to expand the editorial board by opening it to historians from other Soviet republics. Here, however, she met with no success, as the TsK, extremely anxious to keep its eyes on developments at *VI*, refused to approve any of the "republican" names she submitted. Perhaps she should have seen this rebuff as a harbinger of troubles yet to come.

---

ee. quiet (calm) period
ff. hard currency.

With some small previews in the fall of 1954, criticisms of Pankratova's editorial leadership began to be heard from the TsK in 1955. Much of them had to do with her choice of personnel—whom she hired and whom she fired—and with the board's acceptance or rejection of the submissions of authors, though in the latter case the content of the submissions was of course paramount. Those who were fired and those whose work was rejected had evidently taken their complaints to higher authorities, specifically the scholarship section (*Otdel nauki i kul'tury*) of the TsK. Though he fails to elaborate, Kan, as a witness to all this (and, along with his father, as someone who was singled out by the authorities for severe criticism), maintains that the *Otdel nauki* was motivated by what it held to be Pankratova's excessive employment of Jews, while another issue was her willingness to hire and publish former political prisoners and scholars who had undergone political denunciation (the two categories sometimes overlapped). She and Burdzhalov were also accused of acting high-handedly, that is, without full consultation with other members of the board.[122] This was undoubtedly to some extent true; they were, after all, engaged in combat, and some board members turned out to be in cahoots with her political enemies.

Feisty as she could be, especially when her superiors had yet to adopt a clear course, Pankratova was not afraid to engage the *Otdel nauki* in verbal combat. Subjected to severe criticism by the *Otdel* in the spring of 1955, she responded in May with a letter to the top, that is, to Comrades Khrushchev, Pospelov, and Suslov, together comprising the TsK's Secretariat.[123] By way of defending herself, Pankratova related to the Secretariat her version of what had transpired since her appointment as editor-in-chief. After listing the many official and academic burdens she had to carry even while serving in that capacity and naming the many *non*-editorial functions that came with the position (attending and speaking at teachers' conferences, readers' conferences, and the like), Pankratova insisted that the journal had improved enormously and in many respects since she took it over, while at the same time granting, with characteristic modesty, that there was still much to be done and expressing her desire to hear the constructive criticism of the *Otdel*. Alas, she complained bitterly, instead of constructive advice, members of the *Otdel* had recently organized a special conference (28 April) on activities at *VI* in which they intended to subject her and her colleagues to attacks using "impermissible methods that had been condemned by the Party."[124] By this she clearly had in mind the denunciations and accusations that had characterized Soviet academic life under Stalin, methods that Khrushchev had (still cautiously) begun to subject to criticism.

Continuing her narrative, Pankratova complained that just prior to the conference, she was summoned to the *Otdel* for a special meeting where she was for the first time shown a "tendentious" memorandum (*zapiska*) signed by the historian Pavel Volobuev, then an employee of the *Otdel*, in which her work at the journal was sharply criticized on the basis of materials supposedly gathered by an investigatory commission of which she had never even heard and which certainly had never met with her, Burdzhalov, or any of their section chiefs.[125] Pankratova condemned this attempt to "discredit" (*oporochit'*) the editorial board as a declaration of "no-confidence" (*nedoverie*) in the board and "in herself personally" (*k sebe lichno*) and as no way to treat "comrades," even those who are about to be dismissed from their posts.[126] Conceding that a few of the memorandum's criticisms (mainly minor ones) were not without merit—such verbal concessions were part of a long-standing ritual by now—she went on to attack most of its claims point by point, and concluded by describing the "memorandum *signed by Volobuev*" (my emphasis, to indicate a possible suggestion by Pankratova that Volobuev was not the true author) as an "attempt to mislead" (*vvodit' v zabluzhdenie*) the TsK. She wisely signed her letter as "Chlen TsK KPSS" (member of the Central Committee).[127]

Appended to Pankratova's letter was a very long, equally angry "Spravka,"[gg] in which, using the same spirited language, she refuted the charges in even greater detail, with very specific reference to the articles the memo had singled out for harsh criticism by "distorting" their content, and very specific refutations of its charges against individuals she had hired as staff personnel (*nauchnye sotrudniki*).[128]

Whether or not Khrushchev took a serious interest in the controversy soon after reading Pankratova's letter we cannot say. (None of this is mentioned in his memoirs.) But he certainly failed to rein in the *Otdel nauki*, at least not right away. On 17 June, while granting that the Volobuev memo had been wrong on some specifics, a statement from the *Otdel* continued its unrelenting attacks on Pankratova and her journal, even resorting to such tried and true methods as accusing her of working closely with the former "Trotskyite" V. V. Al'tman (true), now her chief assistant at *VI*, and of providing personal assistance to all kinds of recently rehabilitated former

---

gg. supporting material

"Bukharinites" and otherwise politically compromised scholars and writers (equally true). Even her past role in the controversy over *Istoriia Kazakhskoi SSSR* was brought out against her, as was an excessively positive evaluation of Winston Churchill in her 1945 volume of the *Istoriia diplomatii*. This last point was connected with another charge, already leveled in the Volobuev memo and repeated now in connection with her preparations for the forthcoming Xth International Historians' Congress in Rome (August 1955), namely her positive attitude toward foreign historians, not only from the capitalist West, but even from the Peoples' Democracies.[129,hh]

Yet another statement by the *Otdel* dated 27 July was softer in *tone* than its predecessor, but no less critical of Pankratova's performance. By August, however, there was a noticeable change in direction, attributed by Kan, whose information seems reliable, to the intervention of Khrushchev himself, and possibly connected—either as cause or effect—to Pankratova's designation as head of the Soviet delegation to the Rome Congress, the first international historians' congress attended by a Soviet delegation since 1933 (Warsaw), and her election while in Rome to the Bureau of that prestigious body. By mid-August the *Otdel* was expressing itself defensively, criticizing the original Volobuev memo for its excesses, and praising at least some of the accomplishments of the *VI* under Pankratova's leadership. Pankratova, in turn, again acknowledged certain of the least provocative criticisms, paving the way for what appeared to be a peaceful resolution of the conflict.[130]

Against this background, and energized by her very encouraging reception at the International Congress and especially by her reception in February 1956 at the Communist Party's XXth Congress, which she addressed in behalf of the country's historians with Khrushchev's personal approval,[131,ii] Pankratova boldly continued her liberalizing policies at the journal, including the publication of two of Burdzhalov's most controversial pieces, articles that clearly placed Stalin's behavior in March-April 1917 in a negative light, showing his accommodating views toward the "bourgeois" Provisional Government to be similar to Kamenev's, and pointedly challenged the reliability of Stalin's *Short Course*. Pankratova did this

---

hh. Author's note in footnote 129: [*I may say more about this in my final draft.*]

ii. Author's note in the text: [*add a few key quotes from her speech*] See "Anna Pankratova's Speech at the XXth Party Congress," following this paper, for excerpts from the speech.

unaware that shortly after the Party Congress, still many months before such traumatic events as the Hungarian uprising, disturbances in Poland, and the Suez crisis, important leaders of the Party, fearful, no doubt, of the full implications of Khrushchev's secret speech and wishing to stem the tide of liberalization, would renew their attacks on her and her journal.

One precipitant of the Party's retreat from the more robust positions regarding Stalin taken in February at the XXth Congress, at least as this affected Pankratova, was surely the unexpectedly powerful responses to Khrushchev's talk, heard at a series of meetings with the public that were aimed at interpreting the critique of the cult of personality. In Leningrad Pankratova—not unexpectedly, given her major speech at the Congress and her membership in both the TsK and the Supreme Soviet—was asked to play a leading role in the organization of such meetings and lectured at no less than nine of them in the course of only three days, March 21 through March 23. According to Kathleen Smith, Pankratova's audiences at these meetings, held at what Smith suggests was the high point of tolerance of free public discussion of the issues raised by Khrushchev, added up to over 6,000 people, members of what Pankratova herself described as the "Leningrad intelligentsia," mainly writers, scholars, students, schoolteachers, archivists, and local Party activists in search of guidance as to the meaning of the new and still very murky Party line.[132] In her report about these meetings, Pankratova was amazingly frank as to the sensitive questions raised by her listeners, many of which can only be described as provocative. In addition to the questions emphasized by Smith, some of which, as she points out, were of a practical nature (e.g., students of Party history worrying about what to say now in their exams and dissertations), many came precariously close to the edge of the envelope when they raised such dicey topics as Kirov's assassination, the criminal nature of Stalin's misconduct, the failure of the TsK to act against Stalin earlier, the need to revise Party history, and the persistence of anti-Semitism.[133] Although the tone of Pankratova's report on these responses was not untroubled, it could easily lend itself to a reading that suggested that she shared many of their concerns, and it is especially revealing that she saw the responses that addressed the past failures of Soviet historiography as a vindication of the direction in which she had been taking her journal (and was continuing to take it by encouraging and publishing Burdzhalov at precisely this time).[134] For Party stalwarts, including the top leadership, the situation seemed to be getting out of hand.

The attacks on Pankratova by Party circles became fully evident by summertime, when a series of well-orchestrated articles in *Kommunist, Partiinaia zhizn'*, and *Pravda* criticized *VI*, and especially the recent articles by Burdzhalov. Similar attacks were taking place at meetings of Party cells in the academic institutions of Leningrad (led by Pankratova's old nemesis Comrade Kniazev, co-director of the Institut istorii KPSS) and Moscow, including her own MGU History Faculty. There, *VI* was subjected to such ugly accusations as playing into the hands of the Soviet Union's capitalist, imperialist, foreign enemies and defending Trotskyism, while Pankratova found fewer and fewer defenders as time went by.[135] At first Pankratova was cocky enough to fire back at her opponents, including a personal letter to Khrushchev in which she rebutted a letter vilifying Burdzhalov that she knew Kniazev and one of his colleagues had sent to the First Secretary. In her letter and elsewhere, perhaps naively, she accused her enemies of violating the spirit and letter of the decisions of the XXth Party Congress, thereby assigning *herself* the role of defender of the Party's official line.[136] But this time Khrushchev failed to come to her defense, and as the stream of attacks became a flood, Pankratova showed signs of losing her stomach for the fight.

By October 1956 the main venue for the attacks on *VI* that had been building up in Party publications and elsewhere had become the Academy of Social Sciences' Party History Faculty (*Kafedra istorii KPSS*), several members of which had already served as harsh critics of *VI* in those publications (*Kommunist, Partiinaia zhizn', Pravda*, etc.). In contrast to the relatively independent Academy of Sciences, the Academy of *Social* Sciences was, of course, an organ of the Party's Central Committee, and any thought of its adopting a posture toward *VI* that distinguished it significantly from the TsK's current way of thinking had to be precluded.

Beginning on October 16 and continuing on the 23rd and 31st of that month, the *Kafedra* conducted three long and deadly serious discussion sessions devoted entirely to *VI*, especially the articles on Party history in its most recent issues. From the very outset, there was little effort to conceal the evident purpose of these gatherings: to put Pankratova, Burdzhalov, and their colleagues on the defensive and produce a serious change of course in the direction of the journal, especially with respect to the field of Party history.[137] All sessions were closed to the public, including people with professional standing who were not members of the *Kafedra*. The editorial board of *VI* was represented by Pankratova (who was too ill to attend the third session, where she was scheduled to take the floor), Burdzhalov, and two other members, though one of the two was there in the capacity of accuser rather than defender. In addition to faculty members, the *Kafedra's* advanced graduate students were invited to attend, several of whom took an active part in the verbal assaults on the journal and its editors.[ji]

The tone of *VI*'s critics varied considerably. In some cases they spoke very harshly, in a style that might be described as Stalinist-lite—"lite" because they stopped short of accusations of deliberate wrecking, sabotage, espionage, or outright Trotskyism, but "Stalinist" in their clear suggestions that Pankratova, Burdzhalov, and others had been soft on Menshevism, Trotskyism, or at times "Menshevism-Trotskyism," had violated the canons of Leninism and distorted Lenin's views, had gone too far in their critique of Stalin's conduct (especially by conflating it with Kamenev's), had maligned the Party, minimized its achievements, and misstated its positions in early 1917, and had provided ammunition to the foreign enemies of the Soviet Union and Communism, however unintentionally. Others were less harsh in that they conceded, whether grudgingly or with a certain degree of enthusiasm, that despite its errors *VI* had made important contributions to scholarship under Pankratova's leadership. To some extent the critics found themselves trapped by the fact that the XXth Congress's attack on the cult of personality was still in force, which compelled some speakers to agree with *VI* that Party history had been falsified under Stalin and was therefore in need of serious revision, even if *VI*'s revisions had crossed the line from *partiinost'* into *ob"ektivizm* (objectivism), a cardinal sin, and thereby become a danger to the Party. Similarly, both Pankratova and Burdzhalov were trapped by Khrushchev's and the Party's ongoing commitment to the cult of *Lenin*, which compelled them to couch many of their verbal counterpunches in the limiting language of Leninist orthodoxy, at times turning the debate at the sessions into

---

jj. Author's note in the text: [*This section will be expanded by about five pages in order to illustrate both the content and the tone of the speeches, including Burdzhalov's detailed and quite spirited defense of his own articles and of the journal's policies (second session, pp. 88-99) as well as Pankratova's forceful but measured rebuttal to her critics in the form of a letter, read aloud to the third session by one of her critics! (pp. 153-57) and the daring speech by Frug, the sessions' only other vocal defender of the journal (session 2, pp. 56-63).*].
See "Discussions Concerning *Voprosy istorii*, October 1956," for excerpts from the transcript.

another battle of quotations (especially with regard to the dating of Lenin's notion of worker-peasant alliance), and which sometimes weakened their case.[kk] In the end, however, the character of the meeting was never in doubt. The speakers' list was stacked against Pankratova and her colleagues. And though no one referred to this directly, the tension of the atmosphere was surely increased by awareness of the brewing crisis in Hungary, where street demonstrations were peaking just on the eve of the second session. At the conclusion of the third and final session, after the previous speakers had belittled Pankratova's letter for failing to respond to the main points raised by her critics and questioned her competence to serve as editor of the journal, V. M. Donskoi, the chairman of the proceedings, announced that the criticisms of *VI* that had accumulated at the sessions would be transmitted to the TsK.[138,ll]

By early February 1957, citing her deteriorating health and the "acute decline of her capacity for work" (*rabotosposobnost'*), Pankratova requested a leave of absence from her duties at *VI*.[139] By now the weakened heart patient had seen the writing on the wall, and was prepared to accept the inevitable, meaning the radical reconstitution of the editorial board, including the removal of Burdzhalov, the enemy's main prey. The final blow fell on Pankratova in March 1957, when Suslov and Pospelov, almost certainly with Khrushchev's approval,[140] engineered the reorganization of *VI*'s editorial board, the official removal of Burdzhalov, and the de facto elimination of Pankratova, who in any case was fatally ill. Yet despite her depleted physical and moral condition, in one of her rare overt acts of direct defiance of her Party superiors, Pankratova made a quiet, passive, but meaningful parting gesture: she refrained from submitting her resignation as editor-in-chief. On 21 May, lying in a hospital bed four days before her death, she signed off on the long-delayed March issue of her journal, in which the new editors had submissively acknowledged the mindless accusations that had been brought against their predecessors.[141] The possibility, believed by the very responsible German historian Joachim Hösler, that she did something to hasten her own death, cannot be ruled out.[142]

---

kk. Author's note in the text: [Quotes from the stenographic record will be added to illustrate all these points.]

ll. Author's note in the text: [To be added here: a brief discussion of further debates that took place in December.]

In the Nicolaevsky Collection of the Hoover Archive sits a seventeen-page Russian typescript by Boris Nicolaevsky, the great Menshevik scholar and activist, in which, writing on the occasion of Pankratova's death (reported in *Pravda* on 27 May 1957), he attempted to make sense of her career, and especially of her role in the *VI* affair.[143] Nicolaevsky aptly terms Pankratova's life a "personal tragedy," a term that already invests it with a certain amount of dignity. Yet he goes on to pay the subject of his essay only the most grudging respect. She was never a great scholar, he writes, but was more of an organizer of scholarship. Nor was she the kind of person who attracted the warm feelings of others. Her personal appeal was lessened by her devotion to *partiinost'*, which he attributed more to her "careerism" than to her convictions. All her life, he continues, Pankratova strove to follow the Party line, to walk a tightrope, but the line changed so often and so sharply that she was unable to follow all its twists. She took Khrushchev's "new course," his thaw, which proved to be nothing more than a "temporary maneuver," much too seriously, and was unable to follow the rapid shifts in direction that ensued. To be sure, Pankratova's life was very interesting, he continues, not because of her contributions to scholarship, but because of the ways in which, as if in a mirror, her life reflects the story of the internal development and internal contradictions of Soviet Communism and, especially, of Soviet historical scholarship. Later he shifts to a slightly different image, asserting that whatever light had shined from Pankratova was light borrowed from the Party, and did not in any way reflect her personal qualities. Those qualities, corrupted by her education in the school of Stalinism, could not rise to the needs of the times. Hence in the end, he writes, almost as if describing a suicide, her best escape was death, which freed her from the hopeless situation in which she found herself near the end of her life.

Writing as he was without the benefit of the memoirs, diaries, letters, and other documents that have become available over the past fifteen years, Nicolaevsky painted a plausible enough portrait of her life. Evidence for all the characteristics he described—her opportunism, her *partiinost'*, her sacrifice of scholarly for organizational achievement, her naiveté about breakthroughs in the old ways of the Party—can easily be found, and you have seen enough of this in my paper. But it is my contention that such negative characteristics take on a different shape when viewed in their historical and human contexts, when we stand closer to the object of study and watch her making the choices she had—or didn't have—to make. Was

Pankratova really so lacking in principles that we cannot discern any consistency in her ideas and in her actions? Certainly she believed in the Revolution, which I suppose means that she believed in the sanctity of the Party régime that it brought to power. She worked within that system as most people work within the political parameters they are faced with, and with rare (but interesting) exceptions she would never defy a clear decision of her superiors once it had been made. But the rulers of that system, its owners, if you will, were rarely very sure themselves of the course they wished to take or how to go about it, an uncertainty that, at least in the area of historical scholarship, left its practitioners, especially the more daring, with room to maneuver from zig to zag, and Pankratova maneuvered frequently within that space.

With all her zigging and zagging, Pankratova still presents us with a certain degree of intellectual and moral certainty. For one, she was really, not just opportunistically, an internationalist, identifying, if one wishes to a stretch a point by using language she would never have used, with the Westerner rather than the Slavophile tradition in Russian culture. Travel abroad, foreign contacts, and foreign languages were things that she loved, and she looked back at her ethnically mixed Odessa days with pleasure, remaining in close touch with her relatives there.[144] Though hardly rootless, she was indeed a cosmopolitan, and if she inherited anything useful from Lenin it was a healthy distrust of what he and she (and, incidentally, Nicolaevsky) scornfully dubbed "Great Russian chauvinism." This was no mere abstraction for her, but a concrete commitment for which she was willing to put herself at risk more than once, and especially in her relations with her Kazakh colleagues. (Here it might be noted that while her mentor Pokrovskii himself had no personal interest in writing ethno-national-minority histories, he too opposed the introduction of Russian national motifs and supported the protection of national minorities.) How much choice one had in asserting this kind of value of course depended on the political situation, and in this case it was the war itself with its attendant contradictions that opened the door to Pankratova's little crusade. Note, however, that even as the valorization of Russianness grew ever more acceptable (and cruder) in the postwar years, Pankratova was standing up for the traditions of the Chechens and Daghastanis. Of course this meant that, under Stalinist conditions, she could not avoid repeating some watered-down version of the lesser-evil system or even trumpeting the progressive nature of Russia's annexations. This was and had to be a question of emphasis. Pankratova's emphasis was clear.

If we think about them carefully, the historiographical debates in which she engaged, ugly as they were because of the Stalinist ethos of denunciation and character assassination, and simplistic as they often were because of the ritualistic yet plastic discourses of "Marxism-Leninism" (whatever that really was as a "methodology"!), entailed issues that any serious historian would have to engage and that did not lend themselves to easy visions of right and wrong. Most of us non-Marxist historians are usually critical of Pokrovskii and his kind of history for essentially the reasons that were given by his detractors in the 1930s: too abstract, dogmatic, schematic; lacking in flesh-and-blood human agents; neglecting the role of the individual; not sufficiently attentive to Russian historical peculiarities; lacking in the narrative or aesthetic color that we love to find in the historians we most admire. But surely we are also critical of the kind of history that replaced it: too much emphasis on the great man, too many special Russian virtues, to the point sometimes of writing ultra-nationalist history, excessively glorifying Russian military victories and the military and state-building accomplishments of patriotic, heroic, national political leaders (would you be happy, Gertrude Himmelfarb?). I suppose we would have liked our historians to be national, but not too national, with a worldwide perspective, but one that understood and celebrated difference. Were these kinds of issues, carried to extremes, of course, very different from those that divided Soviet historians, at least at certain times? The main difference was the ability of political authority to have the last word in deciding these controversies and the use of physical coercion as an academic weapon, as well as the chilling effect of the historian's knowledge of that potential. Pankratova, in at least three major episodes in her life, pushed the envelope as far as she could without bringing about her own destruction. She had close calls and she had (almost) nine lives. No true, unadulterated opportunist would have let it get that close that many times. In addition, she could assert her independence, such as it was, in small but significant ways, such as her refusal to publicly use the still obligatory term "social fascist" during her European trip in early 1933.[145]

Yes, she engaged in some denunciation herself, and some of it was ugly. Perhaps the ugliest was her treatment of her husband (though the fate of her daughter if she had had to follow him to the GULAG had to have been a serious consideration) and her retrospective treatment of her mentor. But her husband was already a lost cause and Pokrovskii was already dead several years before she fully joined his posthumous tormentors. Later in life, she expressed deep regret for what she had said about Pokrovskii.[mm] As far as I can gather all her subsequent denunciations, by which I mean in this case turning to higher political authorities with complaints against academic colleagues, were defensive in nature, attempts to protect herself and colleagues from ruthless attacks that were themselves political. On the other hand, her life was studded with acts of generosity—I have not included them all in my text, but they are well documented—both moral and financial, to personal friends and colleagues in need, especially those who had been victimized or whose spouses or parents had been victimized by the Terror or by the regime's more garden-variety repressions. This took the form of money (Pankratova generally enjoyed high salaries, for which she worked her tail off), shelter, finding jobs, and just plain stroking, as we now call it. The memoirists and others who have memorialized her have stressed this quality and her personal concern for others. There was probably no way Nicolaevsky could have been aware of this aspect of her life while in exile.

So how should we talk about Pankratova? Apart from assessing her scholarly contributions, and I think they were at least somewhat greater than Nicolaevsky allows—her burdensome life, poor health, and extreme overcommitment prevented her from writing more than one posthumously published volume of her dreamed-of life work, a four-volume history of the Russian proletariat[146]—I think we should imagine her as neither devil or angel, but as someone who did some harm and also much good as she tried to steer a course through the rough seas of Soviet life in a world she could never have imagined as a schoolgirl in Odessa.

This draft was last modified by the author on April 13, 2004. It is reproduced unchanged, with the following exceptions: The author's editorial comments have been moved from the body of the text to the footnotes, and numbered references to other works now appear in the endnotes; all incomplete citations have been completed; several missing citations have been added; typos and minor errors have been corrected. The manuscript opened with the following note: "Draft. Please do not cite or reproduce without permission from the author. 3 sections will be expanded by a few pages each: 1) Pankratova's involvement with Gorky in the "Istoriia fabrik i zavodov" project in the 1930s; 2) her role in the conflict over the history of the Kazakh SSR during World War

mm. Author's note in the text: [find the quote!] Attempts to find this quote have proven unsuccessful.

II; and 3) her involvement in the Burdzhalov affair and the temporary liberalization of *Voprosy istorii* in 1954-6. In addition, the unpublished, unappreciative evaluation of Pankratova's career by Boris Nicolaevsky on the occasion of her death may be used as an opening device instead of being used in the conclusion."

NOTES

1. *Istorik i vremia: 20—50-e gody XX veka. A. M. Pankratova*, ed. Iu. S. Kukushkin, Iu. I. Kir'ianov, et al. (Moscow: Izdatel'stvo RUDN and Izdatel'stvo "Mosgorarkhiv," 2000); hereafter cited as *Istorik*. An earlier collection of recollections by colleagues and comrades of Pankratova (followed by sections on two other Communist women), *Zhenshchiny-revoliutsionery i uchenye*, ed. I. I. Mints and A. P. Nenarokov (Moscow: "Nauka," 1982), pp. 5-80, is much shorter, much less ambitious, and avoids the more interesting and controversial aspects of Pankratova's life. Although the earlier collection contains some useful information, some of it in memoirs by some of the same authors who contributed to *Istorik*, the differences in tone and candor between the two volumes is striking, and is a measure of the distance traveled by Russian academia in the eighteen years that separate them. To give just an obvious example, it would be impossible to tell from the earlier volume that Pankratova began her political career as an SR.
2. My early biographical information is culled from a variety of sources, including the various Party *ankety* (forms), *zaiavleniia* (petitions), and "autobiographies" written by Pankratova in the 1920s and reprinted in *Istorik*, pp. 190-198, and a 1932 "autobiography" reprinted in *Zhenshchiny-revoliutsionery*, pp. 5-8; see also S. I. Potolov, "Nachalo puti," in *Istorik*, p. 23.
3. M. G. Pankratova, "Istorik i vremia," in *Istorik*, p. 20.
4. In a 1923 official declaration, Anna identifies herself as an *intelligentka*; Ibid., p. 196.
5. "Niura Palich's" activities in the Odessa revolutionary underground during the Civil War are discussed with a familiar kind of political enthusiasm and adulation in memoirs of her Odessa comrades (Khana Toporovskaia, Pavel Kitaigorodskii, Betia Bichman, Ol'ga Edel'shtein) in *Zhenshchiny-revoliutsionery*, pp. 57-75. On her undercover work in a *molochnaia* (dairy bar) and her Party assignment in the Moldovanskii district see Kh. S. Toporovskaia, "Nas sdruzhilo podpol'e," Ibid., pp. 57, 59. In later years, when writing to the comrades of her youth Pankratova continued to sign off her letters as "Niura."
6. The early years of these institutions are described and carefully analyzed in Michael David-Fox, *Revolution of the Mind* (Ithaca, 1997). Chapter 3, his chapter on the IKP, provides us with an excellent sense of the environment in which Pankratova carried out her graduate studies and then her professorial duties.
7. Pokrovskii studied with Kliuchevskii as both an undergraduate and (for two years) graduate student, but broke with him after Kliuchevskii expressed disappointment with his Master's thesis. See Robert F. Byrnes, *V. O. Kliuchevskii, Historian of Russia* (Bloomington, 1973), pp. 73, 132, 218; T. Emmons, "Kliuchevskii i ego ucheniki," *Voprosy istorii* (October 1990): pp. 45-61. For the most comprehensive and informative study of Pokrovskii's career, see George M. Enteen, *The Soviet Scholar-Bureaucrat: M. N. Pokrovskii and the Society of Marxist Historians* (University Park: Pennsylvania State University Press, 1978).
8. L. V. Badia, "Etapy tvorcheskogo puti," in *Istorik*, p. 12.

9. Pankratova, *Fabzavkomy Rossii v bor'be za sotsialisticheskuiu fabriku*, ed. M. N. Pokrovskii (Moscow, 1923).

10. Pankratova apparently had a decent command of German; she claimed to have worked hard studying "foreign languages" during her student years at the IKP (Pankratova, "Moi put' k nauke" [8 March 1939], in *Istorik*, p. 215).

11. Pankratova's personal and professional correspondence is laced with references to her medical troubles, which often kept her in bed for extensive periods and forced her to go periodically to convalescence homes (*kurorty*) in Germany (before 1933) as well as in Russia. Her problems seem to have included bouts with nervous depression, from which she invariably bounced back but to which she just as invariably returned. There is a reference to Pankratova's acting as a "superb mother" to her nieces in the memoir of her family friend and former graduate student L. V. Maksakova, "Uchitel' i chelovek," *Istorik*, p. 159.

12. As quoted in " '*Gotova podchinit'sia liubomu resheniiu partii . . .*'(dva pis'ma A. M. Pankratovoi 1937 g.)," *Otechestvennye arkhivy* No. 3 (1999), pp. 64-65 (introductory article by A. N. Artizova); see also Badia, "Etapy," p. 13.

13. In the daughter's carefully chosen words, her parents separated because "they evaluated Stalin differently" (*po-raznomu*); M. G. Pankratova, "Istorik i vremia," p. 21. In her earlier memoir of her mother, "Mat', uchitel', drug" (in *Zhenshchiny-revoliutsionery*, pp. 76-80), Maia makes no reference to her father whatever.

14. David-Fox, *Revolution of the Mind*, especially pp. 169-191.

15. Enteen, *The Soviet Scholar-Bureaucrat: M. N. Pokrovskii*, p. 66, has characterized Zaidel' as "Pokrovskii's arm in Leningrad."

16. For specific examples from 1927-28, see Franco Venturi, "Evgenij Victorovi_ Tarle," in idem, *Historiens du XXe siècle* (Geneva: Librarie Droz, 1966), p. 130.

17. Pankratova, "Moi put' k nauke," p. 215.

18. See N. S. Shtakel'berg, "'Kruzhok molodykh istorikov' i 'Akademicheskoe delo'," in *In memoriam: Istoricheskii sbornik pamiati F. F. Perchenka*, ed. A. I. Dobkin and M. Iu. Sorokina (Moscow: Feniks-Atheneum: 1995), 19-77. See also B. V. Anan'ich, "O vospominaniiakh N. S. Shtakel'berg," loc. cit., pp. 77-86, for an excellent analysis of the links between the "circle of young historians," their professors, and the "Petersburg School" of historiography. As one Tarle specialist has recently put it, Presniakov and Tarle were appealing to the younger generation of budding historians because, in contrast to Platonov, they were "able to find a mode of coexistence with the new régime, combining the traditions of academic 'bourgeois' scholarship with elements of Marxism in its 'moderate,' scientific variant"; B. S. Kaganovich, *Evgenii Viktorovich Tarle i peterburgskaia shkola istorikov* (St. Petersburg: Izdatel'stvo "Dmitrii Bulanin," 1995), p. 33. This kind of fellow-traveling Marxism is precisely what annoyed the left Communist Pokrovskii.

19. Konstantine F. Shteppa, *Russian Historians and the Soviet State* (New Brunswick: Rutgers University Press, 1962), Chs. 3 and 4. For thorough discussions of the Akademichskoe delo, the Pokrovskii-inspired, OGPU-engineered assault on the Academy of Sciences that centered on Platonov's and Tarle's alleged role in an international, monarchist, anti-Soviet conspiracy, see *Akademicheskoe delo 1929-1931 gg.*, ed. V. P. Leonov et al., Vyp. 1, *Delo po obvineniiu akademika S. F. Platonova* (St. Petersburg: Biblioteka Rossiiskoi Akademii Nauk [RAN], 1993), Vyp. 2, and *Delo po obvineniiu akademika E. V. Tarle*, Parts 1-2 (St. Petersburg: RAN, 1998). See also Loren R. Graham, *The Soviet Academy of Sciences and the*

Communist Party, 1927-1932 (Princeton: Princeton University Press, 1967), Ch. 4; and Alexander Vucinich, *Empire of Knowledge: The Academy of Sciences of the USSR (1917-1970)* (Berkeley: University of California Press, 1984), pp. 123- 129. Pokrovskii's 1927 attacks on Tarle et al. are noted in "Predislovie," *Akademicheskoe delo*, Vyp. 2, Part 1, XLVII-XLVIII. The *Akademicheskoe delo* volumes include excellent biographies of Platonov and Tarle that place their arrests and interrogations in the context of their careers. The volumes also include hundreds of pages of testimony by Platonov, Tarle, and others that make interesting reading, though the truth value of such testimony under the conditions in which it was extracted is of course minute. Tarle, for one, ended by retracting most of his testimony. For a fascinating analysis of Platonov's testimony and how it was extracted, twisted, and exploited by his OGPU interrogators, see B. V. Anan'ich and V. M. Paneiakh, "Prinuditel'noe 'soavtorstvo' (K vykhodu v svet sbornika dokumentov "Akademichskoe delo 1929 -1931 gg.' Vyp. 1)," in *In memoriam*, pp. 87-111.

20. See Badia, "Etapy," p. 12, and Pankratova's and G. S. Zaidel's letters to Pokrovskii, 14 and 24 March 1927, in *Istorik*, pp. 269-271.

21. "Predislovie," *Akademicheskoe delo*, Vyp. 2, LII n. On the arrest and exile of Got'e, who was accused of being the plotters' counterrevolutionary chieftain in Moscow, see Terence Emmons, "Got'e and his Diary," in idem, trans. and ed., *Time of Troubles: The Diary of Iurii Vladimirovich Got'e* (Princeton: Princeton University Press, 1988), pp. 22-23.

22. For Druzhinin's fascinating account of his arrest, interrogations, and release, see N. M. Druzhinin, "Moi aresty v 1918-1930 godakh" [1978-79], in idem, *Izbrannye trudy: Vospominaniia, mysli, opyt istorika*, ed. S. S. Dmitriev (Moscow, 1990), pp. 95-102.

23. See Shtakel'berg, "Kruzhok."

24. "Vypiska iz protokola zasedaniia TsKK i NK RKI," in *Istorik*, p. 199; and P. O. Gorin to Secretariat of the Central Committee, 21 April 1931, in Ibid., p. 201.

25. Pokrovskii to Molotov, 5 Feb. 1931, in *Istorik*, p. 201. For the term *delo Pankratovoi*, see Pokrovskii to Moscow Oblast' Committee of the Communist Party, 17 Jan. 1931, in Ibid., p. 200.

26. P. O. Gorin to Secretariat of the Central Committee, 21 April 1931, in Ibid., p. 201. In this memo Gorin, another fellow *ikapist*, wrote: "[Her] persecution reached such proportions that Comrade Pankratova came down with nervous illness [*nervno zabolela*] and was sent to a sanatorium."

27. This is a tentative conclusion based on the absence of any such evidence in the volumes of *Akademicheskoe delo* published thus far. Zaidel's role is noted in "Predislovie," *Akademicheskoe delo*, Vyp. 2, XLVIII; "Evgenii Viktorovich Tarle," loc. cit., XCVII; and Anan'ich, "O vospominaniiakh," p. 85. See also Venturi, "Evgenij Victorovi_ Tarle," p. 131, 131 n.

28. See Enteen, *The Soviet Scholar-Bureaucrat: M. N. Pokrovskii*, pp. 98, 114. More broadly on the conference, see Ibid., Ch. 6; and Shteppa, *Russian Historians and the Soviet State*, pp. 50-53.

29. Enteen, *M. N. Pokrovskii*, pp. 5-6, and Chs. 8-9, passim. Enteen refers to Lazar Kaganovich as Iaroslavskii's "patron" (p. 120).

30. See Ibid., Ch. 6, especially pp. 93-94.

31. Letter dated 26 October 1928, in *Istorik*, p. 273.

32. Pankratova to Pokrovskii, 15 January 1932, in *Istorik*, p. 277. For more

examples see several letters in Ibid., pp. 265-277.

33. As quoted in John Barber, *Soviet Historians in Crisis, 1928-32* (London: Macmillan, 1981), p. 139.

34. Maksakova, "Uchitel' i chelovek," p. 160. The term *polureabilitatsiia* ("semi-rehabilitation") is used to describe Tarle's situation in 1933-35 in Kaganovich, *Evgenii Viktorovich Tarle*, p. 54. During those years Tarle was reappointed professor at LGU, but not yet restored to his position as Academician; see Ibid., pp. 54-58 for further details on Tarle's improved but still difficult situation in those years. Many of the accused in the Akademicheskoe delo were less fortunate than Tarle. Platonov, for example, after a year and a half in prison and removal of his title of Academician, was exiled to Samara in August 1931 for a term of five years, but died there a broken man in January 1933. Although his scholarly works began to reappear in print in 1937, he was officially rehabilitated, together with his fellow defendants (most of them dead by then), only in 1967. His title of Academician was restored in 1968. See Anan'ich et al., "Sergei Fedorovich Platonov. Biograficheskii ocherk," in *Akademichskoe delo*, Vyp. 1, LXXIII-XXIV; idem, "Predislovie," loc. cit., XLIX; and F. F. Perchenok, "K istorii Akademii nauk: Snova imena i sud'by . . . Spisok repressirovannykh chlenov Akademii nauk," in *In memoriam*, p. 193.

35. Zaidel' was arrested in 1936 as a Trotskyist. Ironically, Zaidel's main accuser was the ever-reliable Emel'ian Iaroslavskii; and Venturi, "Evgenij Victorovi_ Tarle," p. 132. On Lukin (arrested in 1938), see Perchenok, "K istorii Akademii nauk," p. 184. Among the other historians close to Pankratova who fell victim to the 1936-38 terrors were the *ikapisty* N. N. Vanag, Grigorii Fridliand, and Semen Tomsinskii. Arrested in early 1935 and later shot was the once influential Bolshevik intellectual, sometime historian, and director of the Lenin Library (1924-1933), Vladimir I. Nevskii, an "old Bolshevik," revolutionary leader, and head of the Bolshevik Military Organization in 1917, who had worked with Pankratova in putting together the documentary collection on the Revolution of 1905. See M. S. Sitonova, "Publikatorskaia deiatel'nost' po istorii revoliutsii 1905-1907 gg.," in *Istorik*, p. 117; see also Barber, *Soviet Historians in Crisis*, pp. 27-28, and Roy A. Medvedev, *Let History Judge: The Origins and Consequences of Stalinism*, trans. Colleen Taylor (New York: Alfred A. Knopf, 1972), p. 167. Nevskii was "rehabilitated" in 1966; Nancy Whittier Heer, *Politics and History in the Soviet Union* (Cambridge, MA: MIT Press, 1971), p. 175.

36. Maksakova, "Uchitel' i chelovek," p. 160. Maksakova's family lived in Otdykh at the time; her own father, an archivist and a close friend of Pankratova's, was also arrested.

37. A. L. Sidorov, "Iz vospominanii (20-40-e gody)," Istorik, p. 163.

38. "Protokol No. 15 zasedaniia PK IKP istorii," Istorik, p. 212; and "'Gotova podchinit'sia'," (Artizova's introduction), pp. 64-65.

39. See "Bibliografiia trudov Akademika A. M. Pankratovoi," in *Iz istorii rabochego klassa i revoliutionnogo dvizheniia: Pamiati akademika Anny Mikhailovny Pankratovoi, Sbornik statei*, ed. V. V. Al'tman, et al. (Moscow: AN SSSR, 1958), pp. 53-70.

40. *Protiv istoricheskoi kontseptsii M. N. Pokrovskogo* (Moscow: AN SSSR, 1939), which begins with Pankratova's own sixty-five-page attack on Pokrovskii's views, and *Protiv antimarksistskikh kontseptsii M. N. Pokrovskogo* (Moscow: AN SSSR,

1940). In addition, she contributed anti-Pokrovskii pieces to *Moskovskii bol'shevik* and other periodicals.

41. The letters, located in the Tsentral'nyi arkhiv Federal'noi sluzhby bezopasnosti Rossiiskoi Federatsii (the Central Archive of the Federal Security Service of the Russian Federation), are part of the files of the "criminal" investigation of E. K. Sokolovskaia. The letters may be found in "'Gotova podchinit'sia'," pp. 66-68.

42. Pages 125-165 of *Zhenshchiny-revoliutsionery* are devoted to memoirs of Sokolovskaia, mainly to her career as a young revolutionary, but with some reference to her subsequent film career. In 1919 Pankratova collaborated with Sokolovskaia on the underground newspaper *Odesskii kommunist*; both served on the paper's editorial board; P. V. Kitaigorodskii, "My rabotali vmeste," in *Zhenshchiny-revoliutsionery*, p. 68; Zh. P. Timchenko, "Legendarnaia Elena," loc. cit., p. 134.

43. "'Gotova podchinit'sia'," p. 66.

44. Ibid. Here and in what follows, all underlining was in the original letters.

45. Ibid., pp. 66-67.

46. Ibid., p. 67.

47. Ibid. All subsequent citations from this letter are from the same page.

48. This is not the place to rehash the ongoing discussion about "speaking Bolshevik," first launched by Stephen Kotkin in *Magnetic Mountain: Stalinism as a Civilization* (Berkeley: University of California Press, 1995), except to say that, to the extent that Pankratova did speak that "language," the point is not so much that she adapted it to her needs as that she grew into it almost artlessly in the course of her youthful evolution.

49. On Pankratova's time in Saratov, see especially G. D. Burdei, "A. M. Pankratova —professor Saratovskogo universiteta v 1937-1940 gg.," *Istorik*, pp. 74-75.

50. Sokolovskaia (along with her husband Ia. A. Iakovlev, head of the TsK's Agricultural Section, the Commissar of Agriculture during and after the collectivization period) had been arrested in December 1937, accused of being a French spy—she had lived in France and spoke French fluently—and a "right-Trotskyist" terrorist; "'Gotova podchinit'sia'," p. 64; and Medvedev, *Let History Judge*, pp. 233, 357, 406. Although the year of her death is correctly stated as 1938, there is no mention of Sokolovskaia's arrest and execution in the forty pages devoted to her in the 1982 collection, *Zhenshchiny-revoliutsionery*. Nor does the volume's brief summary of her husband's stellar Party career (pp. 183-184, note 27) manage to mention his unhappy fate.

51. Basing himself on stories he has heard from people who knew Pankratova well, but also voicing some healthy skepticism, the historian Artizov has raised the possibility that the person who interfered to save Pankratova from a worse fate during the Terror was none other than Nikita Khrushchev ("'Gotova podchinit'sia'," p. 65).

52. Badia, "Etapy," p. 13. In effect, Pankratova was crowned queen of the labor history field when she gave her special address on labor history at the First Congress of Marxist Historians in December 1929, as noted above.

53. For a documentary introduction to what the project was all about, including a key statement by Pankratova addressed to the Warsaw meeting of the VIIth International Congress of Historians in August 1933, see *A. M. Gor'kii i sozdanie istorii fabrik i zavodov: Sbornik dokumentov i materialov v pomoshch' rabotaiushchim nad istoriei fabrik i zavodov SSSR*, comp. L. M. Zak and S. S. Zimina (Moscow, 1959). Pankratova's Warsaw report is on pp. 135-166

(reprinted from *Bor'ba klassov* [No. 10, 1933]). Another valuable work is S. V. Zhuravlev, Fenomen *"Istorii fabrik i zavodov": Gor'kovskoe nachinanie v kontekste epokhi 1930-kh godov* (Moscow: Institut rossiiskoi istorii RAN, 1997). Much less scholarly in its editorial commentaries, but also containing some important documents (including several key statements by Gorky as well as Pankratova's Warsaw speech), is *Sozdadim istoriiu zavodov Leningrada*, ed. and comp. M. D. Rozanov (Leningrad: Lenizdat, 1958), published as an effort to resuscitate the then defunct Gorky project after the XXth Party Congress.

54. Pankratova to Pokrovskii, 1 Nov. 1931, *Istorik*, p. 276.

55. Gorky's statement was published in *Pravda* and other papers. It is reprinted in *Gor'kii i sozdanie*, 25-30 (quote is from p. 30); see also *Sozdadim istoriiu*, pp. 43-48.

56. Pankratova to Gorky, 10 Oct. 1931, in *Gor'kii i sozdanie*, pp. 80-81. For the TsK's official approval of the *Istfab* project see Ibid., p. 31, and *Sozdadim istoriiu*, p. 39. "Pankratova's *detishche*" is used to describe *Istoriia proletariata* by Badia, in "Etapy," p. 13.

57. For the full text of Pankratova's Warsaw report, see *Gor'kii i sozdanie*, pp. 135-166 (object/subject statement on pp. 143-244); also in *Sozdadim istoriiu*, pp. 97-116. Contemptuous of the German factory histories (*Betriebsmonografien*) of the previous three decades, Pankratova dismissed them as capitalist apologetics; she was somewhat less dismissive of representatives of the German Historical School and other German scholars (*Gor'kii i sozdanie*, pp. 150-154). On her participation in the Warsaw Congress, see also O. I. Velichko, "O zarubezhnykh izdaniiakh rabot A. M. Pankratovoi, in *Istorik*, pp. 149-150.

58. *Gor'kii i sozdanie*, p. 144 (see also pp. 149-150, 156-157).

59. Not surprisingly (given the ordeal Ukraine had just experienced during the famine years), the project of compiling factory histories there in the mid-1930s was unsuccessful. See, for example, Gorky's 1933 and 1934 complaints to P. P. Postyshev and N. N. Popov in *Gor'kii i sozdanie*, pp. 232-234. In voicing his complaint against the Ukrainian editorial committee of *Istfab* and the performance of the Ukrainian branch of the Writers' Union (now fulfilling the functions originally carried out by RAAP), he called the Ukrainian endeavor "the weakest, most backward and disorganized" part of the program (p. 232).

60. S. N. Antonova, "Slovo ob uchitele," *Istorik*, p. 153. Antonova was a third-year student enrolled in Pankratova's *spetsseminar* (specialty seminar) at the time.

61. She was actually first assigned this task before the German attack on the USSR, probably in 1940 or late 1939, hence during the Nazi-Soviet pact (N. M. Druzhinin, "Vospominaniia ob Anne Mikhailovne Pankratovoi," in idem., *Izbrannye*, p. 240. The volume, published in 1945, covered the years 1918-1939. Naturally, changed conditions after June 1941 also changed the thrust of the book.

62. This wartime mood is very ably depicted in David Brandenberger, *National Bolshevism: Stalinist Mass Culture and the Formation of Modern Russian National Identity*, 1931-1956 (Cambridge, MA: Harvard University Press, 2002), Chs. 7-9. See also Maureen Perrie, *The Cult of Ivan the Terrible in Stalin's Russia* (New York: Palgrave, 2001). Eisenstein's *Ivan* had of course been anticipated by his *Aleksandr Nevskii* (1938). The prewar antecedents to the new emphasis on the glories of the Russian past, especially in literature and the arts, are analyzed by Brandenberger, Chs. 5-6, where he shows how thin was the line between propaganda works that were meant to glorify state-building and the feelings of national

pride such works generated among their consumers.

63. On the "lesser evil" thesis, first broached in late 1936, see Konstantin F. Shteppa, "The Lesser Evil Formula," in Cyril E. Black, ed., *Rewriting Russian History*, 2nd rev. ed. (New York: Vintage Books, 1962), pp. 107-120 (reprinted as Ch. 11 of Shteppa, *Russian Historians*); Brandenberger, *National Bolshevism*, pp. 50-51, 282 n28, 315 n36. Shteppa's otherwise useful article underestimates the role of the lesser-evil formula during the war years. Brandenberger convincingly attributes the original 1936 formulation of the "lesser evil" thesis to Andrei Zhdanov, not Stalin, as is sometimes claimed.

64. For the field of ethnography, for example, especially with reference to the immediate postwar years, see Yuri Slezkine, *Arctic Mirrors: Russia and the Small Peoples of the North* (Ithaca: Cornell University Press), pp. 303-323.

65. Efimov's dissertation was titled *K istorii kapitalizma v SShA* (Moscow, 1934).

66. Most notably in his major work, *Reguliarnoe gosudarstvo Petra I* (Moscow, 1943). See Nicholas V. Riasanovsky, *The Image of Peter the Great* (New York: Oxford University Press, 1992); see also Black, pp. 244-245, 250.

67. My discussion of Pankratova's views on these matters draws heavily on relevant archival documents published in *Istorik*, pp. 222-236. Of these the most important is her lengthy letter of complaint of 12 May 1944, preserved in the archives of the Academy of Sciences, addressed to the Party's Central Committee, and specifically to Stalin, Andrei Zhdanov, Malenkov, and A. S. Shcherbakov (pp. 228-236). For developments in May-June 1944, I also draw on her two detailed letters to unnamed friends ("Dorogie druz'ia!") and former students, the first dated 15 June 1944, the second undated but probably written in the last days of the same month; one of these friends, the historian Anastasiia V. Fokht, made the letters available to the historian Iurii F. Ivanov, who published them with his notes and commentary as "Pis'ma Anny Mikhailovny Pankratovoi," *Voprosy istorii* No. 11 (1988), pp. 54-79. For more on the wartime conflicts between "bourgeois nationalist" historians and people like Pankratova, see Brandenberger, *National Bolshevism*, Ch. 7.

68. Pankratova to Aleksandrov et al., *Istorik*, pp. 222-223.

69. The article in question was "Sovetskaia istoricheskaia nauka za 25 let i zadachi istorikov v usloviiakh Velikoi Otechestvennoi voiny," Pankratova's introduction to the volume *Sovetskaia istoricheskaia nauka za 25 let*, ed. V. P. Volgin, E. V. Tarle, and A. M. Pankratova (Moscow: Akademiia Nauk, 1942), pp. 3-40.

70. Ibid., pp. 7-9, 12. Of Solov'ev, Pankratova wrote that despite his failure to free himself from "statist" theory, his *Istoriia Rossii* remains to this day a "fundamental collection of the richest, most scientifically reliable [*nauchno proverennyi*] concrete historical material, with historical judgments and connections that were, to a large extent accurately established" (all quotes on Solov'ev from p. 7; quotes on Kliuchevskii from p. 8).

71. Ibid., pp. 13, 34-35 (names listed on p. 35). As Brandenberger points out, Stalin's list of heroic names was constantly invoked in the press and elsewhere in the course of the war; Brandenberger, *National Bolshevism*, pp. 118-119, 312 n14.

72. See, for example, Pankratova, "Sovetskaia istoricheskaia nauka," pp. 31, 37.

73. *Istorik*, p. 223. Pankratova's article was of course replete with praise of Lenin's and Stalin's contributions to historiography.

74. Pankratova, "Sovetskaia istoricheskaia nauka," pp. 9, 13, and 36 (where she

chides her former mentor for having belittled "our traditions").

75. *Istoriia Kazakhskoi SSSR s drevneishikh vremen do nashikh dnei*, ed. M. Abdykalykov and A. M. Pankratova (Alma-Ata, 1943). Abdykalykov was first *obkom* secretary; the presence of his name as co-editor had political as well as scholarly significance.

76. Brandenberger, *National Bolshevism*, especially pp. 121-132; Peter A. Blitstein, "Stalin's Nations: Soviet Nationality Policy between Planning and Primordialism, 1936-1953" (unpublished doctoral dissertation, University of California at Berkeley, 1999), Ch. 2.

77. Druzhinin, "Evakuatsiia iz Moskvy v 1941-1943 gg." [1981]; *Izbrannye*, pp. 228-34, "Vospominaniia ob Anne Mikhailovne Pankratovoi" [1977]; *Izbrannye*, pp. 240-246, especially pp. 242-245; and "Vospominaniia o E. B. Bekmakhanove," *Izbrannye*, pp. 253-259, especially pp. 253-256. Another useful source, though itself partly based on Druzhinin, is N. E. Bekmakhanova, "A. M. Pankratova i izuchenie istorii narodov SSSR," *Istorik*, pp. 170-173; see also idem, "O rabote Mikhaila Porfir'evicha Viatkina v gody evakuatsii v Kazakhstane, v Alma-Ate," in *M. P. Viatkin: Uchenyi, Chelovek, Uchitel'. K stoletiiu so dnia rozhdeniia*, ed. S. I. Potolov (St. Petersburg: "Nestor," 1996), pp. 57-63. Nailia Bekmakhanova is the daughter of Ermukhan Bekmakhanov, a Kazakh historian whose important (and unhappy) role in this story is briefly discussed below.

78. This according to Bekmakhanova, "O rabote," p. 58 (as recounted to her by her mother, one of the participants in these events).

79. Druzhinin, "Evakuatsiia iz Moskvy v 1941-1943," pp. 253-254; Bekmakhanova, "A. M. Pankratova," pp. 172-173; idem, "O rabote."

80. On Viatkin and his distinguished career, see the collection of memoirs edited by his former student Sergei Potolov: *M. P. Viatkin* (cited in full above, note 77). Viatkin had been active in the field of Kazakh history since the 1930s.

81. For a more detailed and nuanced exposition of this debate, see Blitstein, "Stalin's Nations," pp. 36-49.

82. Druzhinin, "Vospominaniia o Pankratovoi," p. 244.

83. Blitstein, "Stalin's Nations," pp. 29-30.

84. Ibid., pp. 21-22.

85. Blitstein, "Stalin's Nations," pp. 32-33. As Blitstein points out, however, even Tarle felt obliged to make some positive comments about rebels like Shamil'; it was common for each side in these debates to make a small bow in the direction of its opponents' position, since *no one* wished to be seen as either insufficiently Marxist or insufficiently "Russian." One good touchstone of the evolution of Tarle's wartime position on Russian national themes is a comparison of his treatment of Generals Kutuzov and Suvorov in the different editions of his prize-winning biography *Napoleon* (first edition, 1936, followed by editions in 1939, 1940, 1941, and 1942). The complicated story of the reception and revisions of that book, including the protective role of Stalin, is well told in Kaganovich, *Tarle*, pp. 58-65. See also the discussion of Tarle's *Nashestvie Napoleona na Rossiiu. 1812 god* (1938, 1939, 1940, 1941, 1942) in Ibid., pp. 66-71, and of his *Krymskaia voina* (vol. 1, 1941, 1944; vol. 2, 1943, 1945), pp. 74-79.

86. That the term "anti-Russian book" (*kniga antirusskaia*) was used is recalled by Druzhinin in "Vospominaniia o E. B. Bekmakhanove," p. 256. Iakovlev had recently published a controversial monograph, *Kholopy i kholopstvo v*

Moskovskom gosudarstve XVII v. (Moscow, 1943), which Pankratova later criticized for its alleged affinity with the "bourgeois-historical" statist approach to history ("Pis'ma . . . Pankratovoi," p. 62).

87. Pankratova to A. A. Zhdanov, dated simply "February 1944," *Istorik*, pp. 223-227.

88. Ibid., pp. 226-227.

89. Pankratova to Zhdanov, 26 Apr. 1944, *Istorik*, pp. 227-228.

90. Pankratova to TsK VKP/b/, 12 May 1944, *Istorik*, pp. 228-36.

91. Ibid., pp. 231. Pankratova goes on to give several other examples, both from scholarship and from the arts (e.g., Aleksei Tolstoi's theatrical representation of Ivan IV; the depiction of Alexander I in the film *Kutuzov*). Eisenstein, as already noted, was an evacuee to Alma-Ata whose stay there overlapped with Pankratova's. Among the other important representatives of the theater and art worlds who were there at the time, housed like some of the historians at the Kazakhstan Hotel, was the great dancer Galina Ulanova. Bekmakhanova, "O rabote," p. 58.

92. *Istorik*, p. 235.

93. "Novye dokumenty o soveshchanii istorikov v TsK VKP(b) (1944 g.)," prepared for publication, annotated, and introduced by I. V. Il'ina, *Voprosy istorii*, No. 1 (1991), pp. 188-205. The actual text of the memorandum and its two addenda is on pp. 190-204. In the discussion that follows, in part for economy of expression, I will refer to the authors of the memorandum simply as Aleksandrov, clearly its prime mover.

94. Ibid., pp. 197-200. This section of the memorandum simultaneously attacks the volume *Ocherki po istorii Bashkirii*, which had recently been published by the Academy of Sciences' Institute of History. Although the attack on *Ocherki* is less personalized than the attack on *Istoriia*, the language of the memorandum is directed against both books, a point I will not repeat in my text. NB: Henceforth I will insert page references to this memo into my text.

95. The conference is astutely analyzed by Blitstein, "Stalin's Nations," pp. 37-43, who makes excellent use of the conference protocols (in *Voprosy istorii* 2 [1996]). Badia, "Etapy," p. 17, dates the first session to 18 May, but this dating is not consistent with other sources, and clearly reflects her misreading of an ambiguous sentence in I. V. Il'ina's introduction to "Novye dokumenty," p. 188, where "18 May" appears to refer to the opening day, but actually refers to a memorandum written eleven days earlier.

96. This point is made by Iu. F. Ivanov in his introduction to "Pis'ma . . . Pankratovoi," p. 54. But it must be added that Malenkov's and Andreev's attendance was sporadic.

97. Pankratova's words, written on 15 June, midway through the conference, while trying to regain her strength at the Uzkoe sanatorium; "Pis'ma . . . Pankratovoi," p. 56.

98. Tarle's words as cited in Badia, "Etapy," p. 16. My references to Pankratova's feelings about the participants and the proceedings are based on the letters to friends in "Pis'ma . . . Pankratovoi." Her reports, which cover the first four sessions of the conference (29 May, 1, 5, and 22 June), give a much more detailed account of her views of the conduct of individual participants than I am including here. Essentially, although the negative personal comments are phrased more harshly, her line of argument in the reports sent to her friends parallels the line in her letters to Zhdanov and to the TsK. On her encounters with Tarle at the conference, see "Pis'ma . . . Pankratovoi," pp. 71, 73; for her snide remarks on his initial absence, her certainty regarding his pernicious role in this affair, and

her condemnation of Tarle for his apologetics regarding the expansion of tsarist Russia, see especially Ibid., pp. 56-58 (comparison to Pokrovskii on p. 57). Although Pankratova and Druzhinin had written a rather favorable review of volume 1 of Tarle's (Stalin) prize-winning *Krymskaia voina* in 1943 (*Istoricheskii zhurnal*, No. 7), they turned against him in print in the months following the conference, taking him to task, for example, for his alleged glorification of Nicholas I's government in his second volume (*Istoricheskii zhurnal*, No. 12, review by Druzhinin); see Kaganovich, *Tarle*, 77.

99. For a more (in my view *excessively*) positive evaluation of the conference proceedings, even referring to Pankratova's *victory*, see Ivanov's introduction to "Pis'ma . . . Pankratovoi," especially p. 55.

100. Citations from Badia, "Etapy," pp. 19-20 (note 35); see also Blitstein, "Stalin's Nations," p. 41, and Brandenberger, *National Bolshevism*, p. 317 n60. According to Brandenburg, who has examined the relevant archival documents, one of Pankratova's addressees, a former student (presumably from her Saratov years), had turned the letters over to the Saratov provincial Party Committee, which in turn brought them to the attention of Aleksandrov and the rest of the TsK.

101. Blitstein, "Stalin's Nations," pp. 45-47.

102. Badia, "Etapy," pp. 17, 20 n35 (quotes from note 35, emphasis added).

103. On the later fate of the Kazakh historians, including Abdykalykov, Pankratova's co-editor, and, most seriously, Bekmakhanov, see Druzhinin, "Vospominaniia o Bekmakhanove," pp. 256-259; Bekmakhanova, "O rabote," pp. 60-63; and Blitstein, "Stalin's Nations," pp. 36-37, 63-71. Under Viatkin's supervision, Bekmakhanov went on to complete his doctoral dissertation on Kenesary and the Kazakh struggles of the 1820s to 1840s, depicting them in a positive light, and to publish it as a monograph-*Kazakhstan v 20-40-e gody XIX v.* (1947), edited by Viatkin. Bekmakhanov was the first Central Asian historian to earn a doctorate. By 1950, however, he was under intense criticism for his "bourgeois-nationalist" approach to Kazakh history and Viatkin was chastised for his failure to discourage his student from taking this line. Viatkin, who agreed to recognize his "errors," emerged relatively unscathed, but Bekmakhanov was arrested, shorn of his doctorate, and sent to a camp in Kolyma. "Rehabilitated" in 1953, he (and his family) maintained close relations with Viatkin until the death of Bekmakhanov in 1966. Viatkin died the following year.

104. For an intimate view of the increasingly ominous mood of the Moscow historians' world in which Pankratova functioned in 1949-50, with many references to her, see "Iz dnevnikov Sergeia Sergeevicha Dmitrieva," *Otechestvannaia istoriia* No. 3 (May-June, 1999). pp. 142-69.

105. For an early example of her very solid work in this field, see E. Korol'chuk, "Iz istorii propagandy sredi rabochikh Peterburga v seredine 70-kh godov," *Katorga i ssylka: Istoriko-revoliutsionnyi vestnik* 38 (1928) pp. 7-26.

106. E. A. Korol'chuk, *"Severnyi Soiuz Russkikh Rabochikh" i revoliutsionnoe rabochee dvizhenie 70-kh godov XIX v. v Peterburge* (Leningrad, 1946). For an extensive account of the anti-cosmopolitan campaign as it affected the Soviet academic world, see Vucinich, *Empire of Knowledge*, pp. 210-247; for its effect on historians, see Shteppa, *Russian Historians and the Soviet State*, Ch. 9.

107. *Istoriia zapadno-evropeiskoi filosofii* (Moscow, 1946). Though the book had been awarded a Stalin Prize and its author was made a full member of the

Academy off Sciences, the attack was actually promoted by Stalin himself; it reached its peak at a special meeting of philosophers convoked by the Central Committee in June 1947. For further background and analysis see Ethan M. Pollock, "The Politics of Knowledge: Party, Ideology, and Soviet Science, 1945 -1953" (unpublished doctoral dissertation, University of California at Berkeley, 2000), Ch. 1. Ironically, Aleksandrov, who was the head of Agitprop and Zhdanov's immediate subordinate, had been one of Pankratova's most pitiless critics during the controversies of the war years.

108. My information on the actions against Korol'chuk are taken form the petition cited in the following note and the editors' summary in *Istorik*, p. 244n. Ironically, if anything, it might be argued that Korol'chuk overstated the Northern Union's distance from the Populist intelligentsia and missed some of the more subtle aspects of the two groups' interrelations; see my "Workers and Intelligentsia in the 1870s: The Politics of Sociability," in *Workers and Intelligentsia in Imperial Russia: Realities, Representations, Reflections* (Berkeley, 1999), especially pp. 39-47.

109. Pankratova et al. to Andrianov, 25 Feb. 1950, in *Istorik*, pp. 241-244. Pospelov, soon to be named Academician, was Secretary of the TsK's Institute of Marxism-Leninism; Zhdanov headed the TsK's Science Department (*Otdel nauki*). Druzhinin and Sidorov had both served as *opponenty* (outside referees) at Korol'chuk's dissertation defense, together with the distinguished historian Boris Koz'min.

110. For evidence of Pankratova's continued concern with Korol'chuk's broken career, see her letters to Korol'chuk, *Istorik*, pp. 315-318, 322-326, and those of Pankratova's secretary-assistant, the former Trotskyite political prisoner, V. V. Al'tman, *Istorik*, pp. 336-338. As late as 1956, according to the Leningrad historian Eva Pashkevich, Kniazev, who had since been reappointed director of Leningrad Istpart, was still obstructing Korol'chuk's career and organizing "*demarshi*" against her; Pashkevich to Pankratova, *Istorik*, pp. 251-252. Eventually, Korol'chuk managed to have additional scholarly accomplishments to her credit, most notably her excellent annotated collection of workers' memoirs, *V nachale puti: Vospominaniia peterburgskikh rabochikh, 1872-1897 gg.* (Leningrad, 1975). In her 1979 celebratory but sanitized overview of Pankratova's career, Larisa Badia cites Korol'chuk (by then recently deceased) as one of the people who assisted her in the preparation of her booklet; L. V. Badia, *Akademik A. M. Pankratova - istorik rabochego klassa SSSR* (Leningrad, 1979), p. 11. It will come as no surprise, however, that Badia completely ignores the controversial aspects of Korol'chuk's career and, by extension, Pankratova's role as her defender. At the same time, quoting from letters from Pankratova to Korol'chuk in the latter's personal archive, she mentions in passing, and without any reference to Korol'chuk's serious predicament at the time, that the two historians communicated about Pankratova's research in the early 1950s.

111. See the diary entries of Dmitriev, "Iz dnevnikov," pp. 163-165. The Guseinov case, which also involved the revocation of a Stalin Prize, is discussed briefly in Shteppa, "The Lesser Evil Formula," pp. 110-112, and idem, *Russian Historians*, pp. 278-279.

112. Quoted in L. A. Sidorova, *Ottepel' v istoricheskoi nauke: Sovetskaia istoriografiia pervogo poslestalinskogo desiatiletiia* (Moscow, 1997), p. 16.

113. Pankratova to Polina R. Vainshtein, 24 Oct. 1953, *Istorik*, p. 321: "Eto dlia menia

ogromnaia chest' i radost', i ona vse perekryvaet."

114. Merle Fainsod, "Historiography and Change," in *Contemporary History in the Soviet Mirror*, ed. John Keep and Liliana Brisby (New York: Frederick A. Praeger, 1964), pp. 19-42; S. V. Utechin, "Soviet Historiography after Stalin," Ibid., pp. 117-129; A. M. Nekrich, *Otreshis' ot strakha* (London: Overseas Publications Interchange, 1979), Ch. 5; and, most recently and most archivally based, Joachim Hösler, *Die sowjetische Geschichtswissnschaft 1953 bis 1991: Studien zur Methodologie- und Organisationsgeshchichte* (Munich: Verlag Otto Sagner, 1995), Ch. 3, and L. A. Sidorova, *Ottepel' v istoricheskoi nauke: Sovetskaia istoriografiia pervogo poslestalinskogo desiatiletiia* (Moscow, 1997), with a valuable documentary appendix. See also idem, "'*Voprosy istorii*' akademika A. M. Pankratovoi," *Istorik*, pp. 76-85.

115. Nekrich, *Otreshis' ot strakha*, p. 143.

116. E. N. Burdzhalov, "O taktike bol'shevikov v marte-aprele 1917 goda," *Voprosy istorii* 4 (1956): 38-56 and idem, "Eshche raz o taktike bol'shevikov v marte-aprele 1917 goda," *Voprosy istorii* 8 (1956): 109-114; see also E. N. Burdzhalov, *Russia's Second Revolution: The February 1917 Uprising in Petrograd*, trans. and ed. Donald J. Raleigh (Bloomington, IN: Indiana University Press 1987), especially Raleigh's excellent introduction.

117. In addition to Sidorova's works, cited above, the most informative and up-to-date work on Pankratova's role in the *VI* affair is the article, part memoir, part research study, by Aleksandr S. Kan, "Anna Pankratova i 'Voprosy Istorii,'" *Istorik*, pp. 85-100 (first published in the Italian journal *Storia della Storiograia* 29 [1996]). Kan, a Moscow historian who emigrated to Sweden, was a member of the *VI* editorial board and a strong supporter of Pankratova and Burdzhalov during the events he decries. He was appointed to the board in 1954, replacing his own ill father, S. B. Kan (who as a young cadet had defended the Winter Palace from the Bolsheviks in October 1917, not the best credentials in the context of what was happening). Below I rely quite heavily on his account. Kan is quite critical of Neckrich's version of these events (p. 85).

118. Yuri Slezkine, "N. Ia. Marr and the Origins of Soviet Ethnogenetics," *Slavic Review* 55, No. 4 (1996), pp. 826-862.

119. Pollock, "The Politics of Knowledge"; Vucinich, *Empire of Knowledge*, Ch. 4. Also, N. S. Khrushchev, *Khrushchev Remembers*, introduction, commentary, and notes by Edward Crankshaw. Trans. and ed. by Strobe Talbott (Boston: Little, Brown, 1970), pp. 269-275.

120. Kan, "Anna Pankratova," p. 86.

121 Ibid., p. 88.

122. Ibid., p. 91.

123. The letter, held in the RAN archive, is reprinted as an appendix in Sidorova, *Ottepel'*: "Pankratova Sekretariam TsK KPSS," *Ottepel*, 221-225. It was dated simply "May 1955." Khrushchev, of course, was then First Secretary.

124. Ibid., p. 222.

125. Kan, "Anna Pankratova," (p. 91), confirms the unpleasant role of Volobuev in this affair, but a precise understanding of that role awaits further research. In general, Volobuev had a marvelous record in the years that followed.

126. "Pankratova Sekretariam," p. 223.

127. Ibid., p. 225.

128. The entire Spravka is reprinted in Sidorova, *Ottepel'*, pp. 226-258. It clearly could not have been prepared by Pankratova alone but was the work of many members of the editorial board and the *sotrudniki*.

129. Kan, "Anna Pankratova," p. 92. It was indeed the case that Pankratova was extremely enthusiastic about the forthcoming International Conference, which she took part in with energy and vigor despite her fragile health and the combat she was enduring in Moscow. Druzhinin's memoirs describe her conduct in Rome in considerable detail; *Istoriki* reproduces some of her correspondence with French, American, and other historians that grew out of these meetings.

130. Kan, "Anna Pankratova," p. 93.

131. Ibid., p. 98. Kan's source regarding Khrushchev's personal approval of the choice of Pankratova, apparently against the will of the other Secretaries, was a conversation with Pankratova's daughter, Maia. In Sidorova's words, many scholars, including Pankratova, saw the Congress's decisions as "a guarantee of the freedom of scholarly inquiry" in the future; Sidorova, "'*Voprosy istorii*,'" p. 78. For the text of Pankratova's speech, which addressed sensitive political issues that went well beyond the limits of her views on Soviet historiography, see *XX S"ezd KPSS: Stenograficheskii otchet* (Moscow, 1956), Vol. I, pp. 618-626.

132. Kathleen Smith, "Answering for Khrushchev: Party Representatives and Questions about the Cult of Personality," paper delivered at the annual meeting of the AAASS (Toronto, November 2002), pp. 4, 10 n28, and passim. Smith's excellent paper contains a broad discussion of audience responses to lectures about and readings of Khrushchev's "secret speech" as well as a close analysis of Pankratova's revealing report to Khrushchev and the TsK on the audience responses, written and oral, to her nine lectures (Ibid., pp. 16-22). For that report see "Dokladnaia zapiska akademika AN SSSR Pankratovoi v TsK KPSS ob itogakh vystupleniia v Leningrade s lektsiiami i dokladami na temu: 'XX s"ezd KPSS i zadachi istoricheskoi nauki'," in *Doklad N. S. Khrushcheva o kul'te lichnosti Stalina na XX s"ezde KPSS: Dokumenty*, ed. K. Aimermakher (Moscow, 2002), pp. 432-448. Pankratova's description of her audience as the *leningradskaia intelligentsia* is in her "Conclusions," Ibid., p. 441.

133. See "Dokladnaia zapiska," especially p. 4

134. Ibid., p. 4

135. These and other similar attacks, both published and oral, are nicely summarized in Sidorova, "'*Voprosy istorii*,'" pp. 80-82.

136. Pankratova to Khrushchev, 6 July 1956, reprinted in Sidorova, *Ottepel'*, pp. 258-259.

137. The overall title on the notices to the meetings was "Ob osveshchenii nekotorykh voprosov istorii KPSS na stranitsakh zhurnala '*Voprosy istorii*'." Verbatim or near verbatim stenograms of these sessions are held in the Rossiiskii Gosudarstvennyi Arkhiv Noveishei Istorii (RGANI), f. 5, op. 30. d 142. My citations are from the Stanford Libraries' Microfilm of those documents, MFILM NS 15770, Reel 34, hereafter cited as *Stenogramma Zasedaniia*. I use the consecutive page numbers (1-185) that were penned on the upper right-hand corner of each page, replacing the earlier typed or penned numbers that were crossed out.

138. *Stenogramma Zasedaniia*, p. 185.

139. Pankratova to Secretary of History Section of AN SSSR Academician E. M. Zhukov, 4 February 1957, as quoted in Sidorova, "'*Voprosy istorii*,'" p. 83.

140. In the eyes of Maia Pankratova, Khrushchev "*sdal*" [betrayed] her mother (Kan, "Anna Pankratova," p. 99). This would help explain Khrushchev's reluctance to mention Pankratova in *Khrushchev Remembers*.

141. Sidorova, " '*Voprosy istorii*,' " p. 83.

142. Hösler, *Die sowjetische Geschichtswissnschaft*, p. 49n. Hösler bases his belief on a private communication from the late Jürgen Kuczynski (21 March 1994), the dean of East German labor historians and once a good friend of Pankratova's; Kuczynski, in turn, had heard the suicide version from other friends of Pankratova's, among them Sergei Tiul'panov.

143. "A. M. Pankratova. (1897-1957)," Nicolaevsky Collection, Series 291, Box 776, item 7; internal evidence from Nicolaevsky's citations suggests that it was written very shortly after Pankratova's death, probably in June.

144. See, for example, her old friend Ol'ga Edel'shtein's account of Pankratova's 1953 "rest" trip to Odessa to visit her sister's family and Pankratova's own grandson; O. E. Edel'shtein, "Takoi ona mne zapomnilas'," in *Zhenshchiny-revoliutsionery*, pp. 74-75.

145. See *Istorik*, p. 150.

146. The completed work, published by the Academy of Sciences, was *Formirovanie proletariata v Rossii (XVII-XVIII vv.)* (Moscow, 1963). It was brought to term, as it were, by a special commission that was chaired by Druzhinin, with her former "Trotskyite" secretary serving as "responsible secretary." The commission included her daughter, some of her former friends, her students, and at least one of her former enemies! Ironically, in view of the title, one of Pankratova's criticisms of certain other historians was that they were too eager to find a "proletariat" wherever they looked.

ANNA PANKRATOVA'S SPEECH
AT THE XXth PARTY CONGRESS

Excerpts from the transcript of A. M. Pankratova's speech
at the XXth Party Congress, February 20, 1956.

From *XX S"ezd Kommunisticheskoi partii Sovetskogo Soiuza:
Stenograficheskii otchet* (Moscow: Gospolitizdat, 1956), pages 618-626.
Translated by Yuri Slezkine.

ONE OF OUR MOST IMPORTANT TASKS is to elevate the study of the history
of our great Communist Party to the level of a true science. In this field,
the effects of the cult of personality, which serve as a brake on progressive
scholarly work, are felt particularly strongly. [p. 621]

Our Party historiography is not paying enough attention to the
activities of Lenin's comrades in arms, the Old Bolsheviks. Just think how
many concrete, important details the reminiscences of Old Bolsheviks
would add to our knowledge, how they would enrich our dry, overly
general Party history books with the flavor of the times and the spirit of
real-life experience! ...

Some historians embellish historical events, simplify them, and represent them in a one-sided way, which is to say, incorrectly. They describe the
journey traveled by the Party as one uninterrupted triumphal procession,
without any complications. . . .

Comrade N. S. Khrushchev's speech contained a bold analysis of the
flaws in the functioning of our economy, state, and Party. Whereas the
Party resolutely rejects any attempt to embellish the current state of affairs,
some of our historians do not have the courage to uncover the difficulties
and defects in the Party's past. [p. 622]

It is with tremendous satisfaction that we welcome the appeal contained
in the Central Committee report, presented by Comrade N. S. Khrushchev,
that concrete facts be studied well, that judgments be made truthfully,
without varnish or embellishment, that our entire ideological work proceed
at a high theoretical level and in total opposition to dogmatism and quo-
tation-mongering. The untruthful representation of the past may prevent
our emissaries and friends abroad from making proper use of the valuable

experience of the Communist Party of the Soviet Union. Unfortunately, we are not being sufficiently uncompromising and resolute in our struggle against the various deviations from the Leninist approach to judging historical events, against the manifestations of antihistoricism and simplification, against the updating of the past in the service of present-day needs. . . .

The inability to analyze the social foundations of historical events and the tendency to blame all our failures on the wrecking activities of our enemies or of those described as our enemies, and to attribute all our successes to the talents of individual leaders are common survivals of the cult of personality, to which we should put an end. [p. 623]

Our textbooks and other books on the history of particular peoples of the Soviet Union do almost nothing to expose the national and colonial oppression those people suffered at the hands of Tsarist autocracy. Correctly emphasizing the progressive significance of the incorporation of various peoples into Russia, some authors lose sight of the other side of the issue. Tsarism brought brutal oppression to those peoples and delayed their political, economic, and cultural development. It is well known that Lenin called Tsarist Russia the "prison of the peoples." It was the October Revolution that dismantled that prison. We need to study the history of the national movements within the Russian Empire much more thoroughly. We should study them in their historical specificity, taking into account the full range of internal and external factors and, above all, the attitudes of the popular masses themselves. We should be sensitive to the progressive phenomena in the history of all peoples, large and small, and continue our struggle on two fronts: against great-power chauvinism and against local nationalism, because they are two sides of the same coin. [pp. 623-624]

The Soviet state put an end to the Tsarist policies of annexations and oppression and ushered in a new era in the history of international relations. It is, therefore, incorrect to claim—as some authors do, contrary to statements by Marx, Engels, and Lenin—that the wars of annexation conducted by the Tsarist regime were just wars, or that the Franco-Russian alliance of the late nineteenth century or Tsarist Russia's policies in China were admirable. Such accounts contradict historical facts and make it impossible to understand the revolutionary changes introduced into foreign policy by the Soviet state from the first days of its existence. . . .

The problems in the historical and other social sciences are associated with the defects in the process of training new scholars. All regulations concerning dissertations and academic ranks and titles were made in

1934-35. Thousands of dissertations have been defended over the last two decades and, especially, after the war. Their quality is poor, however. They contain little creative new research but plenty of quotations, standard formulas reproduced verbatim, and occasionally retellings of other texts, with or without quotation marks. [p. 624]

There are a lot of problems in the administration of scholarly work. Among them are instances of formal and bureaucratic attitudes. We write many resolutions and hold many meetings, but we do little scholarly work and conduct few scholarly debates. The Academy of Sciences of the USSR, which has a very large staff, functions as just another bureaucratic institution, without regard for the fact that scholarly work has its own peculiarities and that science cannot be administered in the same way as the economy. [p. 625]

DISCUSSIONS CONCERNING *VOPROSY ISTORII*, OCTOBER 1956

Excerpts from the transcript of the meeting of the Department of Party History, "The Treatment of Certain Questions Concerning the History of the CPSU in the Journal *Voprosy istorii*," held on 16 October, 23 October, and 31 October, 1956 (RGANI, F. 5, op. 30, d. 142).[1]

Translated by Yuri Slezkine.

Comrade Frug:

The Department of Party History did a great thing by getting us together for a discussion of the treatment of certain questions concerning the history of the CPSU [Communist Party of the Soviet Union] in the journal *Voprosy istorii*. We all agree that such an initiative is in accordance with the decisions of the XXth Party Congress on creativity in scholarly work, particularly in the history of our glorious Party. But when I consider Comrade Petrov's presentation, I ask myself: Does such a presentation contribute to the fulfillment of the objectives set before us by the Party, which guides us toward greater creativity in our scholarly work? Does it contribute to a serious discussion and analysis of such an important period in the history of our Party as March and April, 1917? I feel very strongly that it does not, and that in fact it does the opposite.

Voice from the audience: "What's your proof?"

I'll give you proof, although I must say that nobody required proof from Comrade Petrov, for some reason. As I was listening to Comrade Petrov, I was reminded of Herzen's words that ideas that have outlived their usefulness may go on hobbling along for a very long time. It seems to me that a whole set of ideas, big and small, that were spawned by the cult of personality, are now trying to hobble along, leaning on a cane. In his presentation, Comrade Petrov used certain tricks and methods typical of that period, when scholarly discussions were replaced by vicious attacks meant to "finish off" or "break" one's opponent. First of all, we must leave behind such tricks and methods, because they do not help scholarly creativity and do not bring us closer to the truth—they do the opposite.

You ask for proof? I'll give you proof.

When the time came for Comrade Petrov to "finish off" Comrade Burdzhalov, he read a passage from one of his articles from the personality cult era and said: Look what Burdzhalov used to write! And there was laughter in the audience. And I thought to myself: Who are we laughing at? We are laughing at ourselves! Which one of us did not write in that way, which one of us did not talk in that way, which one of us did not feel that way about various periods in our Party's history?

I would like to ask Comrade Petrov if he remembers this book I have in my hand. In this collection, published by the Department of Party History of the Academy of Social Sciences and edited by Professor Kostomarov, there is an article by Comrade Petrov entitled "Comrade Stalin, the Leader of the Sixth Party Congress." [...] I will not cite any other passages from the article that involve direct falsification of the facts, but I will point out that Comrade Petrov writes that the VIth Party Congress adopted Stalin's recommendation that Lenin appear before the court, whereas in fact the Congress rejected Stalin's recommendation and adopted the opposite recommendation: that Lenin not appear before the court. [...] I am not going to reproach you for what you wrote then. I know the conditions that made you say such a thing, or perhaps could lead to honest mistakes being made. But now that we are trying to correct our mistakes, why are you forcing us to go back to what we used to write then? We all made mistakes. The point is not to grant some kind of mutual amnesty, but to correct the mistakes we all made. [ll. 56-58]

Comrade Burdzhalov:

Many of the discussants have made some very valuable comments, but Comrade Petrov's and the second speaker's comments lacked objectivity. Let's assume that, while working on this topic, I got some things wrong or did not answer all the questions fully, but why hang labels on me? I've been accused of objectivism and subjectivism, and of championing the cult of personality in reverse. Who needs all this? We should have a serious discussion and examine things carefully.

Comrade Petrov's objective was not to raise questions for debate, introduce new issues, or move the discussion forward. No, he was looking for instances of falsification. This seems to have made an impression on some comrades, because in such a large forum nobody can figure out which one of us is right. What kind of serious scholarly discussion can we have if my opponent repeatedly misstates my positions? [...]

Of course, every problem in Party history—as well as all research problems—should be approached from the position of Party-mindedness. But what is Party-mindedness as we understand it? It is a truthful, objective record of the events. There should be no contradiction here. We need a truthful history; we must not hide the truth. If some Party leaders or some individual Party members made mistakes or showed hesitation or indecisiveness, why conceal this? The party is big enough not to have to fear such things. What's the point of concealing or of hiding things? We need a real, truthful Party history. [ll. 91, 97]

V. M. Donskoi [chair]

Due to illness, A. M. Pankratova cannot be here, so she has sent us a letter. Comrade Baglikov will proceed to read the letter. [Comrade Baglikov reads the letter.]

Dear Comrades:

For health reasons, I am unable to participate in today's discussion and have to limit myself to writing this letter. I hereby request that my letter be read during the meeting.

The editorial board of *Voprosy istorii* welcomes the discussion of its work by academic departments and other groups of historians. The board has organized and will continue to organize readers' conferences in Moscow and other cities. The discussion of our journal's work in your department is also perfectly legitimate. However, in my view, the first two sessions cannot be considered normal.

According to the agenda, the discussion was to be devoted to articles dealing with Party history. This year, sixty-five articles on the history of the Party and Soviet society have been published in our journal. However, for some reason, the discussion has revolved around an article by E. N. Burdzhalov. The discussion began with an-hour-and-a-half-long presentation by I. Petrov, in which he focused exclusively on this article and misrepresented many of its arguments. Of the other articles, only those by comrades Polevoi, Moskalev, and Iakovlev were mentioned during the discussion. But do other articles not deserve critical consideration? Are there no important issues in the history of the Party that we need to discuss in the light of the decisions of the XXth Party Congress? Unfortunately, most comrades who have participated in the discussion have focused on certain awkward or imprecise formulations, instead of discussing the work of the journal in the light of the decisions of the XXth Party Congress.

I have no intention of commenting on specific factual criticisms of E. N. Burdzhalov's article. The author himself has responded to those criticisms in a way that I find, for the most part, convincing. Some of his arguments require further elaboration, and some critical remarks made by the discussants, particularly the criticisms dealing with the author's description of Bolshevik tactics as being limited to the questions of war and power, strike me as fair. On the whole, however, I believe that the article analyzes the issues correctly and contributes to the overcoming of the cult of personality in our Party historiography. Comrade Petrov and other comrades point out reproachfully that E. Burdzhalov used to write differently. But did not we all, including Comrade Petrov, treat certain historical questions incorrectly, from the position of the cult of personality? So why should we now criticize our comrades for abandoning their old, erroneous positions? Why should we justify positions that I. V. Stalin himself found deeply erroneous? Objectively, I. Petrov is defending the old positions, which were widespread during the era of the cult of personality. Such positions are holding us back. [. . .]

The as yet unstudied and unresolved problems of history can be solved with the help of serious scholarly discussions. The party is calling for scholarly debates, the struggle of opinions in scientific work. It is, therefore, difficult to understand why Comrade Kostomarov attacked our journal for its polemic with Comrade Bugaev's article, published in *Partiinaia zhizn'*. Comrade Kostomarov went so far as to claim that, by publishing that article, we had dared to disagree with the Party's central organs. But does Bugaev's article really express the opinion of the party's Central Committee? One may disagree with our response to Comrade Bugaev, but no one can deny us the right to state our point of view regarding a particular question of historical science. Comrade Kostomarov is accusing us of stirring up discussion all over the country. He does not want any discussions or debates, even as he enjoins us to follow the decisions of the XXth Party Congress.

Comrade Kostomarov spoke against a letter we published about the inadmissibility of distortions in publications of memoirs by Old

Bolsheviks. The letter mentioned two books, one of which was edited by Comrade Kostomarov. In his presentation, Comrade Kostomarov did not say anything about the distortions contained in that book, but he did defend arbitrary abridgments made in the other book, which does not have his name on the cover and with the publication of which he claims to have had nothing to do. However, the official release by the publisher states that Comrade Kostomarov was a scientific consultant and official referee, and that it was in response to his recommendation that Vasil'ev-Iuzhin's memoirs were cut by almost a half. What is curious is that among the omissions (which are not mentioned anywhere) we find not only the names of particular individuals, but whole pages of text that contradict certain arguments made in Comrade Kostomarov's book, *The Moscow Soviet in 1905.* [...] Such treatment of historical sources, including memoirs, is inadmissible; it is sheer falsification. [. . .]

At the present juncture, Soviet historians are facing very important challenges. Reactionary bourgeois elements are not only hatching counterrevolutionary conspiracies and complicating the international situation, but also waging an ideological war in an attempt to weaken the socialist camp and undermine the prestige of the Soviet Union in the world. We must intensify our struggle against bourgeois ideology. To accomplish that, we must develop a genuinely scientific history of the Party as the leading force of the international revolutionary movement. It is imperative that we demonstrate the international significance of Leninism and the role of Lenin as the founder of the Party and the Soviet state and the leader of the laboring masses of all countries; tell the truth about our Party's proletarian internationalism; and popularize the Leninist norms of intra-Party democracy, Leninist principles of relations among Communist parties, and Leninist approaches to relations among different peoples and states. We can meet these challenges only if we fully overcome the cult of Stalin's personality, reject all the distortions and falsifications that were brought about by that cult, and provide a genuinely scientific and truthful coverage of historical events. It is for the achievement of these goals that our historians should be mobilized. [ll. 153-157]

NOTES

1. RGANI is *Rossiiskii gosudarstvennyi arkhiv noveishei istorii*, or the Russian State Archive of Contemporary History. CPSU is the Communist Party of the Soviet Union.

Participants in the discussion included L. S. Frug, I. F. Petrov, G. D Kostomarov, V. T. Baglikov, E. Bugaev, Iu. Z. Polevoi, M. A. Moskalev, and A. I. Iakovlev.

"BEFORE CLASS":
REGINALD ZELNIK AS LABOR HISTORIAN

Laura Engelstein

REGGIE ZELNIK'S WORK ON RUSSIAN LABOR HISTORY revolves around a central guiding theme. It focuses on how it was that people employed in factories came to think of themselves as belonging to the category of worker. He wanted to know how the full scope of their experience, both at work and after hours, induced some of them to engage in collective protests and a few of them to think that radical ideas correctly interpreted their situation. In short, Reggie was interested in the process of class formation.

The question of why it was that working people, individually and collectively, responded to political programs and engaged in organized protests is of course central to all studies of labor history. In the Russian case, it is central to understanding the growth of the Marxist political movement that developed into Bolshevism and the triumph of a regime that claimed to speak for the working masses. European class categories—and later, specifically Marxist concepts of class and class consciousness—entered Russian public discourse in the second half of the nineteenth century, along with the growth of industry and urban centers. These concepts are therefore embedded in the historical record; they influenced the course of events by shaping the terms in which people interpreted the social landscape. They have also influenced the way historians organize their thinking.

Reggie's goal was to separate the historian's perspective from that of the historical actors and also from the particular version of Russian history embodied in Soviet orthodoxy. By examining the process that translates social experience into political commitment, he accepted the assumption that experience and ideology are related, but he did not accept the revolutionary outcome as inevitable. He focused therefore on the earliest stages of worker mobilization, when protest emerged as a direct expression of the workers' sense of grievance, before exposure to radical ideology had provided a conceptual scheme to interpret what they felt. As he wrote in the introduction to *Labor and Society*, he wished to understand "the situation of urban workers independently of the history of revolutionary politics"

(p. 2). He called a later essay "Before Class."[1]

It was not that the history of revolutionary politics escaped his attention. He meticulously charted the process by which radical agitators entered into contact with workers and how workers came to understand the ideas they dispensed. But radicals were not the only outsiders who affected the lives and outlook of workers. Workers also interacted with police, government officials, and establishment professionals. Examining these encounters, Reggie stressed the complexity of the environment in which working people made personal and collective choices. Nor did he treat the workforce as an aggregate or abstraction, but focused rather on the psychology of individual figures. Following a few rank-and-file individuals through the stages of their lives, he traced the pathways by which they came to define themselves in political terms.

Nowadays we would say that his work examined issues of identity, subjectivity, and the cultural construction of social categories. Reggie himself avoided any such language, which has only recently displaced the Marxist cadences that affected even those social historians who rejected Marxist dogmas. Like most labor historians of the 1960s, Reggie accepted the problem of the working class and its political evolution as a real problem. It was a problem that had preoccupied the actors themselves: the people who fit the social description or thought they did, as well as those who wished to stimulate or inhibit labor mobilization. Reggie did not consider the concept of the proletariat to be an illusion perpetrated by intellectuals in pursuit of political aims or a structural grid imposed by the Gods of Discourse. He did, however, see the concept as a social product, a co-production of outsiders and insiders. His focus on process and on the self-activation of the laboring masses put him in the company of E. P. Thompson, whose *Making of the English Working Class* (1963) explored the cultural resources that shaped worker behavior. Reggie's later work was influenced also by the French philosopher Jacques Rancière's *La nuit des prolétaires* (1981). Critical of historians and theorists who treated the working class only in collective terms, Rancière explored the ideas of the few workers educated enough to express them in writing. Separated from their fellows by their cultural achievements, they nevertheless provide the only direct evidence of how workers themselves articulated their values and aspirations. Rancière's insistence on allowing the lowly subjects of history to speak for themselves resonated with Reggie's interest in the self-documentation of worker lives.

Reggie Zelnik
in the early '70s

This interest was not a flight from social issues into the domain of representations. Reggie was interested in "how things seemed," but not from a premature affinity with later deconstructionists. He never doubted that how things had really been could be grasped by ordinary methods of historical analysis. (Not for nothing did he call his affectionate parody of Russian historiography "Wie es eigentlich gegessen."[2]) The "how things seemed" question shows up, rather, as an element in the production of how things actually turned out. He cared about personal psychology, which is where perception and interpretation get their start—in the hearts and minds of individual people. In a similar strategy, which approached the larger picture through its separate parts, he used case studies—what he called "case histories"—to understand broad social trends. Thus, the Kreenholm strike, with all its local features, illuminates the dynamics of labor protest in other settings as well.

Reggie's own thought structure is deeply imbedded in his narrative. His style is deceptively conventional. He was a die-hard empiricist: there was a truth to be found. Who, where, when? What did they read (dates, titles, editions)? What did they have for breakfast, who did they encounter and on which park bench? What was the first time for this or that, what were the particulars? The details are important because they add up: it is the weight of detail that shapes human understanding—both for the actors in the stream of time and for the scholars who piece the story together. For Reggie, the details illuminate a problem, while at the same time blocking the urge to oversimplify: the local, personal, accidental, and inconsistent all contribute to the historical process. In their totality, they amount to a coherent picture, but one that cannot be reduced to a formula of any kind.

Reggie's work demonstrates, in fact, that methodological insights, whether from anthropology, cultural theory, or social science, can inform historical research without overpowering it. The reason he avoided current terminology is not only that he often wrote *avant la lettre*, but because he extracted theoretical insights that helped him formulate questions and interpret his material. His goal was never to illustrate general propositions or validate abstract concepts. His purpose was to understand how the microcosms of place, circumstance, personality, and community interacted to generate the movements of human aspiration and political conflict that animate the past. He never lost the sense of drama and pathos, which depends for its effect on the activation of our moral sensibility and on the recognition that things might have turned out differently, that choice as well as structure have shaped historical events.

There are three landmarks in Reggie's scholarship: *Labor and Society in Tsarist Russia: The Factory Workers of St. Petersburg, 1855-1870* (Stanford, CA: Stanford University Press, 1971); *A Radical Worker in Tsarist Russia: The Autobiography of Semën Ivanovich Kanatchikov* (Stanford: Stanford University Press, 1986); and *Law and Disorder on the Narova River: The Kreenholm Strike of 1872* (Berkeley and Los Angeles: University of California Press, 1995). It is worth examining how they are put together and how Reggie's classic preoccupations evolved over the years.

Labor and Society, which emerged from Reggie's doctoral dissertation, completed in 1966 at Stanford University, was preceded by a handful of articles that highlight some of the book's dominant themes. One shows how recent migrants from the village to the factory, not yet accustomed to the urban or industrial environment, might engage in meaningful acts of collective protest. Essays on the Sunday-school movement of the early 1860s and on the "first encounters" between populist students and industrial workers in the 1870s analyze the effects of exposure to educated mentors. Another essay examines the protests that affected a St. Petersburg machine factory in 1860.[3] In the book, these examples of processes caught at their inception are interwoven with chapters on the social and economic profile of the city and on the attempts by the authorities and the urban elites to confront the emerging industrial economy and its social impact.

One of the book's more powerful insights is the observation that government policies designed to inhibit worker activism eventually promoted the outcome they were supposed to prevent. Paternalistic legislation aimed to preempt worker protest by mitigating the harsh conditions of factory labor. Such regulations, however, not only antagonized industrialists but encouraged the workers to think of themselves as a recognized category. A strike at the Nevsky textile plant demonstrated the new expectations generated by government intervention into labor relations; it showed the workers' capacity to articulate and defend what they came to perceive as their rights. The subsequent trial made manifest the contradictions in official policy that were themselves to exacerbate rather than calm worker discontent: while acknowledging the justice of many of the strikers' claims, the court punished their leaders for breaking the law against collective action.

Labor and Society is not just history "from the bottom up." It is history from all around. It situates the workers, who are the focus of its concern, in the St. Petersburg urban landscape. It describes the moral, professional, and intellectual perspective of the educated groups concerned with problems linked to the emerging factory system (health and disease, conflict and violence, exploitation and justice, ideology and the challenge to authority). Reggie had contemplated a second volume that would have taken the story into the 1870s, when contacts between workers and radical agitators intensified. Instead, he took a detour into another dimension of the labor question. His second major publication, *A Radical Worker*, shifts the focus from groups and structures to the level of the individual life. It also moves forward in time to the years in which industry itself had expanded and the impact of radical ideology had deepened. The book consists of the translated and edited autobiography first published in 1929 by Semën Kanatchikov, a worker who by then identified as a Bolshevik, describing his experiences up until 1905.

The translation was preceded by two hefty articles that analyzed the life presented in this account, alongside that of Matvei Fisher, another worker of the period.[4] Both Kanatchikov and Fisher rose from the ranks to join the revolutionary movement: hence the reference to August Bebel, who began as a laborer and ended as a leader of German Social Democracy. Archival documents, which Reggie later edited for publication, allowed him to trace Kanatchikov's career in Soviet times. In the

1920s, he was a zealous enforcer of the Party line, but in the 1930s fell victim to the purges.[5]

Kanatchikov's memoir describes how he managed to find a place in the social landscape so ably charted in *Labor and Society*. The young man is aware of social and cultural hierarchies. He meets educated people and compares his own abilities and habits to theirs; he compares himself to fellow workers at different levels of intellectual development and adjustment to urban ways. Reflecting back from the perspective of a Soviet journalist, he recounts the classic story of ideological conversion, but does so with an engaging freshness and individuality.

Reggie's next work combined the dimensions separated in the first two. *Law and Disorder on the Narova River: The Kreenholm Strike of 1872* (1995) explores a particular industrial setting—a large textile mill located on the border of St. Petersburg and Narva Provinces, thus also of mixed Russian-speaking and Estonian-speaking populations. It reconstructs the story of how inchoate worker discontent evolved into an organized strike movement. Exploring the general problem of labor mobilization through the prism of a single event, *Law and Disorder* also draws the portrait of an individual participant: the worker Vasilii Gerasimov, who, like Kanatchikov, left a memoir of his early years.

Written in 1881-82 and first published in 1906, fourteen years after the author's death, this account was composed before the worker autobiography had emerged as a specific genre. Unaffected by Bolshevik hindsight, it covers the years before radical organizers had penetrated working-class circles. The Kreenholm episode, Reggie writes, demonstrates "the spontaneous character of Russia's early labor unrest before the exposure of workers to radical ideology and prior to the development by the state of a fixed scheme of classification for such events" (p. 1). The narrative provides access to the process of identity formation "before class," as Reggie puts it. Gerasimov acquires a sense of belonging and purpose not from the encounter with abstract theory, but from the experience of shared hardship and marginality. Nor does he define himself exclusively in relation to his place at work: his background as a Finnish-speaking orphan remains an important point of reference.

In constructing his own scholarly narrative, Reggie believed that "elements of character and contingency should interface with broader structural conditions and constraints" (p. 2). In choosing a "moment of Russian history when the precise rules of engagement in social conflict of this kind had not been codified or ritualized" (p. 5), he focused on the possibilities open to both parties to the confrontation. The workers, he notes, demonstrated an incipient awareness of legality and legal rights. The authorities recognized this impulse and did what they could to respond, yet their inconsistency fed the discontent they hoped to dampen.

The question of the legal context for labor conflict and its impact on the relationship between workers, employers, and the state was a theme Reggie had intended to develop in a broad, comparative framework. He had outlined an ambitious history of strikes, from 1789 to 1917, covering the examples of France and Prussia (later Germany), as well as Russia. In addition to assessing the influence of contrasting legal systems on industrial relations, the study would have traced the way images and attitudes toward strikes migrated from one culture to the other. The goal was to analyze the range of practices and representations over the long nineteenth century (and even potentially into the early Soviet years) across the breadth of continental Europe. An essay on Gerhart Hauptmann's play, *The Weavers,* and its Russian reception provides a taste of what this project would have accomplished.[6]

Reggie's other work in progress was the short biography of Anna Pankratova that appears in this volume. Almost complete at the time of his death, the essay should be understood in the context of his long-standing intellectual preoccupations. Pankratova was not a worker, but a student of workers. A fierce guardian of Soviet orthodoxy, whose scholarly activity promoted the Stalinist version of labor history, Pankratova established her personal identity in this unforgiving professional world. Her case presents Reggie with the inverse of Gerasimov's. The question is not how an intellectual innocent acquires a style of thought, but how a well-trained thinker finds room to maneuver within a prescribed system.

Far from dismissing Pankratova as an inflexible dogmatist, Reggie singles out moments in her career when she took professional risks, deviating, however slightly, from the Party line, as in the early Khrushchev years. Unlike cases of open dissidence or absolute compliance, this example of what he calls "constrained dissent" illustrates the potential for choice available even to people fully integrated into the system, at least in post-Stalin times. Perhaps he strains too hard to absolve Pankratova of subservience. Searching for evidence of moral courage even in such inhospitable circumstances, Reggie demonstrates his own faith in the human capacity for self-assertion and independence of mind. He was him-

self a political activist and he respected contemporaries, as well as historical personalities, who devoted themselves to social causes. He had no
patience, however, for ideological certainties; he believed that political
commitment should embrace argument, skepticism, and personal idiosyn-
crasy. He realized that principled people changed their minds; he changed
his own mind on some subjects. Most of all, he always looked for the grain
of goodness in the least promising of characters, especially if they had in
some way endured oppression themselves. Perhaps it is a stretch to think
of Pankratova, an administrator of orthodoxy, as a victim of the system,
but Reggie allows her some benefit of the doubt.

Reggie's last publication as a labor historian thus reflects on the professional responsibilities of labor history itself. He managed in this case, as
he always had, to combine intellectual rigor with generosity of heart. Alien
to careerism in all its forms, he tried to fathom the inner complexity of a
relentless careerist. His own career began in the era of Khrushchev's
reforms, when international contacts were possible but difficult, and
lasted into the post-Soviet age, when Russian and American colleagues
interact with ever increasing ease and profit. His work has withstood shifts
in scholarly fashion and the end of a political era. His concern for the
meticulous verification of the facts, his interest in the personal experience
behind collective movements, his rejection of easy explanatory schemes, and
his persistent attachment to what remains a central question for Russian
and Soviet history have earned him the enduring respect of Russian, as well
as Western colleagues. His work remains a model of independent thinking
and human empathy.

NOTES

1. "Before Class: The Fostering of a Worker Revolutionary, Construction of His
   Memoir," in *Russian History*, Vol. 20, Nos. 1-4 (1993), pp. 61-80.
2. "Wie Es Eigentlich Gegessen: Some Curious Thoughts on the Role of Borsch in
   Russian History," in *For Want of a Horse: Choice and Chance in History*, ed.
   John M. Merriman (Lexington, MA: Stephen Greene Press, 1985).
3. "The Sunday School Movement in Russia, 1859-1862," in *Journal of Modern
   History*, Vol. 37, No. 2 (June 1965), pp. 151-170; "An Early Case of Labor
   Protest in St. Petersburg: The Aleksandrovsk Machine Works in 1860," in *Slavic
   Review*, Vol. 24, No. 3 (September 1965), pp. 507-520; "The Peasant and the
   Factory," in *The Peasant in Nineteenth-Century Russia*, ed. Wayne Vucinich
   (Stanford, CA: Stanford University Press, 1968); "Populists and Workers: The
   First Encounter Between Populist Students and Industrial Workers in St. Petersburg,

1871-74," in *Soviet Studies*, Vol. 24, No. 2 (October 1972), pp. 251-269.

4. "Russian Bebels: An Introduction to the Memoirs of Semën Kanatchikov and Matvei Fisher," Parts 1 and 2, in *The Russian Review*, Vol. 35, No. 3 (July 1976), pp. 249-289; and Vol. 35, No. 4 (October 1976), pp. 417-447.

5. "The Fate of a Russian Bebel: Semën Ivanovich Kanatchikov, 1905-1940," in *The Carl Beck Papers in Russian and East European Studies*, No. 1105 (University of Pittsburgh, 1995). See also Frederick C. Corney, *Telling October: Memory and the Making of the Bolshevik Revolution* (Ithaca, NY: Cornell University Press, 2004), pp. 150-153.

6. "*Weber* into *Tkachi*: On a Russian Reading of Gerhart Hauptmann's Play *The Weavers*," in *Self and Story in Russian History*, ed. Laura Engelstein and Stephanie Sandler (Ithaca, NY: Cornell University Press, 2000).

IN AND OUT OF CLASS:
REGINALD ZELNIK AS TEACHER AND MENTOR

Benjamin Nathans

REGGIE ZELNIK WAS KNOWN FOR MANY THINGS—his engagement as a
young Berkeley faculty member with the Free Speech Movement, his
pioneering studies of workers and the labor movement in late Imperial
Russia, his fondness for a good bottle of wine—but I would venture that
his greatest legacy at Berkeley and in the field of history lies in his role as
teacher and mentor, understood in the broadest sense. Few historians in
our time have inspired such a large and loyal following and few have been
as publicly recognized for their mentoring, above all at the graduate level.[1]

Over the course of more than three decades, twenty-eight graduate
students completed their doctoral dissertations in Russian history at
Berkeley under Reggie's supervision (see Appendix 1). For other Berkeley
students in a variety of fields, Reggie served as thesis committee member,
seminar teacher, and reader, providing his unique blend of critical engagement, encouragement, and wit. As a former Berkeley graduate student in
the history of science recently said to me, Reggie was open to considering
any argument, any question, and any subject, though he certainly wasn't
reluctant to critique, graciously and insightfully, just about any argument,
any question, and any subject.

At Berkeley, Russian and Soviet history were not a separate subfield;
they were part of the study of Europe. This configuration encouraged
Reggie's students to approach Russia as he did, in a broadly European context. It also set students who came to Berkeley to study West or Central
European history within Reggie's orbit, which in more than one instance
led to a shift of interest to Russia. In fact, Reggie's influence as teacher and
mentor extended well beyond Berkeley. There are a number of people in
the profession today who consider him their mentor even though their
PhDs are from other universities, people whom as graduate students
Reggie took under his wing and whose work he nurtured. The number of
books in whose acknowledgments Reggie is thanked is staggering.

Reggie's combination of open-mindedness and engagement seemed entirely in sync with the Bay Area itself. When I arrived in California to begin graduate school in the fall of 1987, Berkeley was utterly unfamiliar to me, and like many new graduate students I was amazed at how rapidly it became not just familiar but intensely pleasurable. Ocean, sun, and fog conspired to produce the world's ultimate climate control. All the human senses were provided for. Wandering around the campus and its environs one hardly knew where to turn first: Moe's used books? Cafe Roma? The Cheeseboard? Tilden Park, with its fragrant eucalyptus groves and spectacular panoramas of the Golden Gate? More than a playground for adults, the Bay Area seemed to open the mind to itself and to the possibility that things could be done in new ways. The atmosphere in the Berkeley history department had a similar effect. Graduate students immersed themselves in creative disorientation: Linguistic turn? Epistemes? Representations? New Historicism? Theory was everywhere—in our seminars, in our reading groups, in conversations in the corridors of Dwinelle Hall. Not in the middle of it all, but slightly to one side, making sure we learned some history while ingesting all that theory, was Reggie, in black jeans and plaid shirt, more often than not a well-chewed toothpick leaning out of his mouth.

What did Reggie teach, and how did he teach it? Research on history pedagogy confirms what many a college professor has suspected, namely that students typically forget the vast majority of the content of their history courses within a year, and that what remains in their memories is some residue of the teacher's intellectual persona, the rhetorical style, the quality of "presence." The dance critic Arlene Croce once described the residue of a performance as the "afterimage," "the impression retained by the retina of the eye, or by any other organ of sense, of a vivid sensation, after the external cause has been removed."[2] For Reggie's many students, the afterimage is what we are left with when the teaching, and now the teacher himself, are gone.

Reggie was often described as an ideal reader. His written comments on students' work, rendered in numerous marginal notes and marvelous one- or two-page handwritten analyses of a chapter or seminar paper, covered everything from high concept to footnote format. In a history department known for its critical engagement with theory, Reggie taught that it was not enough to be an architect; you had to learn stonecutting too. He had an uncanny ability to detect unresolved problems or doubts in a text, no matter how deeply submerged, yet even his most incisive criticisms managed to offer encouragement. The truly marvelous thing about Reggie's comments, however, was the way they allowed us to see our own work, and sometimes our own selves, in a new light. This was often the necessary first step to rethinking and revising, and ultimately, to that mysterious process known as learning.

In the classroom, as in his own scholarship, Reggie rarely referred explicitly to works of theory. I sensed in him a certain homegrown skepticism vis-à-vis elevated schemes that sought to bring order to vast stretches of human experience but that lacked the messiness and texture of individual lives.[3] And yet when conversations turned to webs of significance, epistemic breaks, public spheres, or cultural capital—fare feasted on by graduate students in my time—it was obvious that Reggie was not only familiar with names like Geertz and Foucault and Habermas and Bourdieu, but had already developed a critical inner dialogue with them. I recall one meeting of a graduate seminar on Soviet history in which a student attempted to "explain" Stalinism as a Foucauldian disciplinary regime, only to have Reggie gently question whether the power/knowledge nexus under Stalin really exhibited the subtle capillary mechanisms that Foucault associated with its modern incarnation. Though I never heard him actually say it, I think Reggie regarded theory as nothing more and nothing less than a tool, an instrument one could use to generate not so much better answers as better questions. A tool was not an explanation.

Like all great teachers, Reggie taught by example. It may sound odd, but the most important things I absorbed from him in his oral teaching mode came not in seminars or lectures but at talks by visiting historians in the department lounge in Dwinelle Hall. I often learned more from the questions Reggie posed, and from the way he posed them, than from the talks themselves. Here was a man who would stand up among his colleagues and students, and without a trace of pretense or posturing, in a spirit both gentle and penetrating, offer gems of questions whose sole purpose seemed to be to help the speaker think beyond the arguments he or she had just presented. Those who believe that the decisive step in any intellectual endeavor is the posing of a good question will appreciate the tremendous value of such moments for Reggie's students.

One cannot describe Reggie's teaching without invoking his sense of humor.[4] My earliest memory of him in the classroom dates from my first week of graduate school, in the opening session of a research seminar on urban identities in late Imperial Russia. The readings were drawn from a book called *The Semiotics of Russian Cultural History*, a challenging work whose purposes evidently did not include calming the nerves of beginning graduate students. Reggie's opening gambit consisted of a brief discourse on the semiotics of the annual conference of the American Association for the Advancement of Slavic Studies, with special attention to the elevators and the hotel bar as well as to the question of why roundtables are not round. It remains to my mind the most insightful analysis of how such conferences actually operate. With hindsight, I have also come to view this episode as emblematic of Reggie's teaching style, which managed to combine a certain mischievous irreverence for the whole racket known as "history" with a genuine commitment, I would say a moral commitment, to exploring the intersection of interiority and behavior in the everyday experiences of living, breathing human beings.

One of Reggie's favorite marginal comments was the suggestion to "flesh out" a certain issue. To flesh out meant to put flesh on, to make more human. Reggie's own scholarship, I believe, reached its most profound moments in its attention to individual human beings like Matvei Fisher, Semën Kanatchikov, Vasilii Gerasimov, and, in the substantial article contained in this volume, Anna Pankratova. In his subfield of labor history, dominated by the category of class, Reggie nonetheless developed a deeply person-centered approach to writing about the past, anchored in the conviction that—as he puts it in his analysis of Pankratova's stormy career—"it is important to understand the role that was played by personal experience," the "human context" in which historical actors lived.[5] Reggie took seriously the postmodern critique of the historical self, but at the end of the day he was not afraid to reflect on the emotions and psychic journeys of individual protagonists.

In this respect scholar and teacher were one, for Reggie's teaching was also highly person-centered. We students felt this. I felt it especially in the questions he posed. When a student was working on a dissertation prospectus, he would ask: What kinds of documents would you like to find in the archives? When an argument rang hollow: Is this really your voice here? Always, there was his attention to voice and language. As he writes in the opening passages of *The Perils of Pankratova*, "How should we be talking about a life like Pankratova's? What is the appropriate language for historians to use and what should be the role of moral assessment in an analysis of this kind of life?"[6]

I know too little of Reggie's education and early career—not to mention his upbringing—to say with any certainty how he arrived at his distinctly person-centered mode of teaching and writing history. Nor do I wish to engage in facile speculation about the impact of certain events and individuals. Nonetheless, it strikes me as impossible to ignore the tremendous significance for Reggie of the Free Speech Movement—a movement about language—that was unfolding at Berkeley just as he joined the history department faculty in the fall of 1964. Twenty-eight years old, he was not quite a real professor, occupying instead a liminal position, as described in a memoir of those years written some four decades later:

> Though a faculty member, I was still a graduate student myself, having not yet finished my Stanford dissertation, and senior faculty [sympathetic to the FSM] may have taken this as an indication of insight into the students' thinking. I had not yet broken the "over thirty" barrier, but more to the point, in the course of our encounters I had developed a personal rapport with some key members of the FSM [. . .] because we could, to various degrees, speak the same political language.[7]

With his hyphenated student-professor identity, Reggie observed and took part in the political roller-coaster ride of the FSM from an unusual vantage point. His perspective found expression in one of his earliest published works, a short essay about faculty-student relations that appeared in the journal *Dissent* in 1966 under the suggestive title "Prodigal Fathers and Existential Sons: A Report from Berkeley." It is not simply that Reggie was thinking about parallels between the FSM and the Russian revolutionary movement—that much is clear from his observation that "the slogan 'when the chips are down the professors cannot be trusted' is as common among the students as similar slogans once were about social-democrats." Rather, what one finds in his writing about Berkeley students and the FSM—at the time as well as much later—is an early version of what would become his characteristic blend of criticism and encouragement. Reggie was fundamentally sympathetic to the students' agenda. More than that, he willingly jeopardized his tenure prospects at Berkeley by publicly supporting the demand for free speech in the university. The university and the country, he wrote, had "something to gain from being morally informed" by "unkempt prophets." But the *Dissent* essay is hardly an encomium for student activism. It notes the "egocentric" character of many politically

Reggie and Elaine Zelnik at Chez Panisse, Berkeley, at the wedding of a close friend in May, 1996.

involved students who "automatically become the center of their own universe." It complains of the "burden" of constant political litmus tests applied by students to the faculty, and of their "increasingly shrill and sometimes unbearable" voices. And yet, it concludes, "if the students ever stop complaining about the university, it may well be a sign that they have abandoned hope. If they stop protesting about American politics, the situation will indeed be hopeless."[8]

Reggie's refusal to stake out easy positions would become one of the hallmarks of his persona as historian and teacher. He was not given to emphatic statements. He knew where his loyalties lay, but he also recognized simplification as an enemy of genuine enlightenment. I suspect that the moral skepticism and intellectual humility that mark his work emerged from a rich dialogue—conducted within himself and with his wife Elaine—about issues of the day, including (but surely predating) the FSM. And I wonder whether from this ongoing conversation there perhaps emerged Reggie's characteristically dialogical relationship with his students, his engaged response to their ideas and their work.

One of those "key members of the FSM" with whom Reggie found a common language was of course Mario Savio. The son of a Sicilian machine-punch operator, Savio was the spellbinding orator whose speech in Sproul Plaza declaring that "There is a time when the operation of the machine becomes so odious ... you've got to put your bodies upon the gears ... you've got to make it stop" captured the movement's spirit. Mario Savio the student and Reggie Zelnik the student-professor became, as Reggie later wrote, "lifelong friends."[9] More than that, though, I would suggest that Savio became "exhibit A" for Reggie's growing conviction that individuals matter in history. As Michael Rossman, an FSM student activist, has written, "For decades the historian Reggie Zelnik and I have argued politely about contingent history. Would there have been an FSM without Mario? There would surely have been something. Reggie thinks it would have been quite different and likely much less effective."[10]

I never heard Reggie speak about Savio or the FSM; he never mentioned them in or out of class during my time as a graduate student. But in an obituary following Savio's death in 1996, he described Savio's significance for the FSM in terms even more pointed than Rossman's:

Writing a century ago, a Russian Marxist maintained that circumstance created Napoleon: had Napoleon not existed, someone else would have filled his shoes. Well, I came to know everyone who might have been Mario if Mario hadn't existed, and I know that only Mario could have done what he did. In three months he turned thousands of students into a united voice for free speech, persuading a complacent faculty to accede to the Free Speech Movement's demands.[11]

For virtually his entire professional career, Reggie carried with him a sense of Savio's unreproducible role in the defining political movement of his (and Reggie's) life. He carried with him as well a lifelong admiration for what he called the "dialogical quality" of Savio's public speeches, which "engaged students at the level of their own apprehensions [...]. They were not being fed dogma but were invited to a forum. Mario was able to personalize and even feminize the idiom of the movement."[12] Suitably adapted to reflect a pedagogic rather than a political context, this sentence may come as close as any to capturing Reggie's own qualities as teacher and mentor.

Reggie's person-centered approach also found expression in his legendary generosity and concern for his students as human beings. In the years since I left Berkeley I have learned what I scarcely sensed then: graduate students are time-consuming. It remains an enigma to me how Reggie managed to give detailed and illuminating comments on so many dissertation chapters, so many articles and manuscripts by colleagues across the country and overseas. In his capacity as academic adviser, Reggie was sure not to neglect the tasks of stonecutting: he paid scrupulous attention to details like funding opportunities for his students, letters of recommendation (and their deadlines!), and job hunting. It again remains an enigma to me how he cheerfully managed to write so many letters for fellowships and jobs, make so many phone calls on our behalf, take so many students out for a celebratory drink after they passed their qualifying exams. There is no need to complete this endless inventory of giving—the hundreds of people who attended the memorial service for Reggie held in Berkeley in August 2004 and the numerous gatherings in his memory at universities and conferences across the country in the months that followed offer their own eloquent testimony.

What then of Reggie's afterimage? A complex man known for many things, he cannot be reduced to a still-life, nor would he have wanted to be. One might describe him as David Vital once described Bernard Lazare, an engagé historian and early defender of Alfred Dreyfus, as "that very great rarity, a man of absolute and uncompromising intellectual integrity, but also one with a consistently and diligently kept open mind."[13] Yet this hardly captures what it felt like to be Reggie's student. In 1996, at a surprise dinner party celebrating the publication of a Festschrift in honor of his sixtieth birthday,[14] I toasted Reggie as the "Un-doktorvater," an advisor who somehow seemed to transcend the emotional baggage of the student- mentor relationship, who possessed an uncanny ability to speak with his students as colleagues-in-the-making. I stand by that description. And yet I must confess that when the shocking news of Reggie's death reached me, I and the other Zelnik students with whom I spoke had an overwhelming feeling of having been orphaned. Dwinelle Hall without Reggie, Berkeley without Reggie, the field of Russian history without Reggie—these are simply unthinkable. We have lost an unforgettable teacher and a magnificent human being.

NOTES

1. In 1996 Reggie shared with the historian Joan Wallach Scott the American Historical Association's Nancy Lyman Roelker Graduate Mentorship Award. For the full award citation, see *Perspectives* (February 1996), pp. 15-16.
2. Arlene Croce, *Afterimages* (New York: Vintage, 1977), p. ix.
3. An early example of this position can be found in Reggie's first book, the introduction to which announces that the author seeks to approach workers' identities "concretely within the context of the flow of Russian history, and not as a reflection of any sociological law of development." See his *Labor and Society in Tsarist Russia: The Factory Workers of St. Petersburg 1855-1870* (Stanford, CA: Stanford University Press, 1971), p. 5.
4. Those who missed Reggie's humor in person can get a taste of it in his essay "Wie Es Eigentlich Gegessen: Some Curious Thoughts on the Role of Borsch in

Russian History," in John Merriman, ed., *For Want of a Horse: Choice and Chance in History* (Lexington, MA: Stephen Greene Press, 1985), pp. 77-89.

5. Reginald E. Zelnik, *Perils of Pankratova*, pp. 36, 63 in this volume.

6. Ibid., p. 13 in this volume.

7. Reginald E. Zelnik, "On the Side of the Angels: The Berkeley Faculty and the FSM," in Robert Cohen and Reginald E. Zelnik, eds., *The Free Speech Movement: Reflections on Berkeley in the 1960s* (Berkeley and Los Angeles: University of California Press, 2002), p. 293.

8. Reginald E. Zelnik, "Prodigal Fathers and Existential Sons: A Report from Berkeley," *Dissent* (May-June 1966), pp. 285-289.

9. Reginald E. Zelnik, "The Avatar of Free Speech," *New York Times Sunday Magazine*, December 29, 1996, p. 34.

10. Michael Rossman, "The 'Rossman Report': A Memoir of Making History," in Cohen and Zelnik, *The Free Speech Movement*, p. 208.

11. Zelnik, "The Avatar of Free Speech," p. 34.

12. Ibid.

13. David Vital, *A People Apart: The Jews in Europe, 1789-1939* (New York: Oxford University Press, 1999), p. 557.

14. Gerald D. Surh and Robert E. Weinberg, eds., *Russian History/Histoire Russe (Festschrift for Reginald E. Zelnik)*, Vol. 23, Nos. 1-4 (1996).

PROFESSION AND POLITICS:
REGINALD ZELNIK AS A CAMPUS LEADER

David A. Hollinger

THE CAMPUS MEMORIAL SERVICE for Reggie Zelnik in Faculty Glade on August 29, 2004, was one of the larger "state funerals" in the history of the University of California at Berkeley. Yet the deceased was not one of Berkeley's chancellors or presidents, nor was he among its football coaches or its Nobel Prize winners. The memorial drew so many hundreds because, as the testimony of speaker after speaker revealed, the assembled current and former faculty, students, administrators, and staff understood this rank-and-file professor to have exemplified the finest qualities of their university. Many of those drawn to The Glade that day also knew Reggie beyond campus as a person of exceptional generosity and integrity. But Reggie was very much a man of the campus, and was among its most conscientious and effective citizens. For forty years he gave and gave and gave to the University of California at Berkeley.

One of the things he gave was reasoned criticism. Reggie was devoted to the University—he "believed in it" in an almost religious sense—but he never felt bound to accept it strictly on its own terms. Rather, he engaged it, defended what he most appreciated about it and worked hard to make it a more worthy place for human beings to learn from one another. He paid it the deep respect of investing his best critical energies in it. To speak of Reggie as a campus figure, complimenting the portraits of him as a teacher and as a historian contributed to this volume by others who knew him, is to invoke a series of institutional contexts in which Reggie applied his superior critical judgment. Unlike many persons of his generation with political commitments on the left, Reggie was not aloof from or even uncomfortable with institutions. He was a vigorously practical as well as a deeply moral man, and understood institutions—especially universities—as potential instruments for good as well as for ill.

Prominent among the specific campus institutions within which Reggie worked were the Institute of Slavic, East European, and Eurasian Studies, the Department of History, and the Academic Senate. Reggie served a term as Director of the Institute (1977-1980), and was on its

108

Executive Committee regularly from 1970 until his death, at which time he was serving this committee as its chair. He attended and contributed to many events sponsored by the Institute. He was a regular participant in some of them, including colloquia and staff parties, and he could always be counted on to take a visiting scholar to lunch or dinner. He was similarly a mainstay of the Department, serving a term as chair (1994-1997) and compiling one of the most imposing records of committee work in departmental memory. He was appreciated for his informal role in mentoring junior faculty in all fields. In the Senate, too, he did more than his share. His most important Senate contribution was probably his service on the 1967 Commission on Governance, a prodigiously time-consuming endeavor that produced one of the longest and most theoretically sophisticated treatises on university governance ever to come out of a committee.[1] Although the Commission's recommendations for sweeping changes in the governance of the campus were eventually rejected by the Academic Senate, and thus disappeared from memory as an anticlimax to a series of campus strikes that had motivated the Senate to join with the student government organization in appointing the Commission, the episode illustrates Reggie's willingness to apply himself to the often thankless task of finding fair solutions to the most vexing and contested of campus issues. Many thought the Commission was doomed from the start, but Reggie, whose resilient capacity for hope was a personal trademark, wanted to give it a chance. He proved to be an energizing and integrating force on the Commission. Those who served with him never forgot his perspicacious interventions in meeting after meeting.

And so it was with the Free Speech Movement, the most widely known of the campus events in which Reggie played a major role. When he spoke, people listened. He was trusted by virtually everyone. The significance of this widespread trust may be lost on anyone lacking a sense of how contentious and often chaotic an atmosphere that was—one in which charges of "sellout" and "anarchist" came easily off the tongues of many faculty and students who in other situations were more charitable to those with whom they disagreed. The trust Reggie won from all parties is even more remarkable given the fact that it was his very first semester on the faculty, and that he held only the title of Acting Assistant Professor because he had not completed his own doctorate, a prerequisite for the rank of Assistant Professor and for voting membership in the Academic Senate.

Reggie maintained close contact with several student leaders of the

FSM, especially Mario Savio, but also Henry Mayer, Michael Rossman, Martin Roysher, and Steve Weissman. These people trusted him because, in part, he convinced them that he cared as much as they did about free speech. I was not a leader of any kind in the FSM, but I shared this feeling about Reggie, whose mixture of sincerity and analytic rigor I appreciated as soon as I witnessed it in the conversations he carried on with students in the hallways of Dwinelle Hall and on "The Terrace," the outdoor section of what is now called the Caesar Chavez Center but was then a gathering place for graduate students to eat lunch and argue politics. In the meantime Reggie was becoming a central figure in the faculty groups who spent November and December of 1964 trying to find solutions to the campus crisis that were consistent with basic FSM goals. The faculty who got to know him in this setting trusted him because, in part, he convinced them that he cared as much as they did about the university.

Reggie was one of a handful of professors able to go back and forth, explaining the concerns of sympathetic faculty to the FSM Steering Committee, and explaining the latter's point of view to faculty who were often frustrated by what they saw as the failure of the students to recognize the complexity of the politics of higher education in the state of California. Roysher recalls a crucial meeting, held in his own apartment, when Reggie and his history colleague Lawrence Levine sought to gain the confidence of the FSM leadership: "I remember the two of them sitting alone on the couch as we arrayed ourselves around the room in an inquisitorial arc that reflected our skepticism that two people hardly older than us could turn around a vaunted faculty."[2]

Reggie's account of the faculty groups sympathetic with the FSM, including his own role in the operation of those groups, is contained within his painstakingly detailed and documented essay, "On the Side of the Angels: The Berkeley Faculty and the FSM." In characterizing his own views, and those of the history colleagues who formed the organizing core of the larger "Committee of 200" that successfully won Academic Senate approval of the legendary pro-FSM resolutions on December 8 of that year, Reggie recalls: "We were all strong civil libertarians and civil rights supporters, and we shared various ideas about how to find a solution to the conflict that would secure free speech and advocacy, preferably without costing the administration a total loss of face."[3] Although Reggie also said he had felt somewhat out of place in the presence of distinguished senior historians such as Carl Schorske and Kenneth Stampp, who brought him into their political circle, their recollections[4] of him as a pivotal figure among faculty supporters of the FSM should remind us that Reggie's narrative, in "On the Side of the Angels," is exceedingly modest, and does not do justice to his own contribution to the mobilization of faculty in support of the December 8 resolutions.

Although Reggie's courageous, judicious, and sensitive behavior during the FSM crisis is an important part of his story as a campus leader, I pass quickly from this famous set of events in order to emphasize a related, multi-year contribution that remains less widely appreciated, and hence invites attention here. Reggie was a vital keeper of the legacy of the FSM, unafraid to disagree with other FSM veterans who wanted to spin it one way or another to meet the needs of later historical moments. His most visible acts as a conscientious custodian of the FSM's place in history were co-editing, with Robert Cohen, *The Free Speech Movement: Reflections on Berkeley in the 1960s*, published in 2002, and writing for that volume his article, "On the Side of the Angels." But he was also in the middle of the negotiations during the late 1990s that led to the creation of the FSM Café in Moffitt Undergraduate Library. In those negotiations Reggie was once again a crucial go-between, making sure that the concerns of Mario Savio's family and friends as well as those of the University Library were addressed candidly and fairly before the private donation that funded the venture could be accepted and put to its designated use. Reggie was also an advisor to the Bancroft Library's ambitious project of FSM oral histories and document collections. He was always one of the first people to get a phone call when any effort was made to mark the place of the FSM in the campus's history.

Reggie's willingness to keep alight the flame of the FSM long after many on campus had lost interest in it has resulted in the association of his name with the FSM, and in obscuring his prominence in other political highlights of Berkeley history, especially within the 1960s. Indeed, Reggie was more important in the antiwar movement than he had been as a supporter of the FSM. As the antiwar movement grew, Reggie, on account of the respect he had earned in 1964, was constantly in demand to preside over potentially contentious meetings, or to serve as a go-between when different groups lost patience with one another. In 1966 it fell to Reggie to moderate a mass meeting at which United Nations Ambassador Arthur Goldberg defended the Vietnam War in a forum that greatly overshadowed the occasion for Goldberg's visiting the campus, his being awarded an

Reggie Zelnik chairing the Vietnam Debate at Harmon Gym, University of California at Berkeley, Spring 1966.

honorary degree at Charter Day. In the face of pressure—including demands from some fainthearted FSM veterans—to keep Goldberg from voicing his unpopular views, Reggie was absolutely determined "that Goldberg be given the opportunity to present his case," as Leon Litwack has written, even in the face of "a hostile audience of some 7,000 in Harmon Gym." Reggie believed, Litwack continues accurately, "that if free speech stands for anything, it is the right of others to speak out on behalf of ideas we find very distasteful or wrong."[5] The crowd kept its peace until Goldberg finished his speech, and then in a straw vote indicated their overwhelming opposition to the war. No one lacking Reggie's formidable moral standing on campus—no one but Reggie himself, one cannot help but be amazed in retrospect—could have stared down that adamantly antiwar crowd as he did, keeping the honor of the campus and of the FSM intact while the Ambassador spoke. That same year Reggie joined with colleagues Peter Dale Scott and Franz Schurmann in writing *The Politics of Escalation in Vietnam,*[6] an important contribution to the antiwar movement nationally and one that cemented Reggie's reputation as a stalwart of the antiwar forces in Berkeley.

Reggie often presided over meetings of the Faculty Peace Committee, a group to which he recruited me during 1967-68, a year in which I held the title of Acting Instructor in the Department of History while working on my doctoral dissertation. This professional title, like Acting Assistant Professor, did not carry voting rights in the Academic Senate, but it was technically a faculty title, and as a result Reggie assured me I was eligible to join this group that was active in opposing the Vietnam War. I remember the tact and subtle humor by which Reggie would try to steer the group to reject the often foolish and fanatical—so many of us thought—proposals of the contingent from the math department, but without offending them. The math group always sat together, in front of the room, and Reggie would sometimes wince when their hands shot up. When one of these more-radical-than-thou mathematicians accused Reggie of being insufficiently militant, I heard him respond with what he represented as a quotation from Lenin to the effect that sometimes in politics, leaders must not take direct action, but must instead "patiently, patiently explain" to their constituency what they need to know with some future action in mind. I have no idea if it really came from Lenin, but I thought the invoking of Lenin was a shrewd way for Reggie, who was not a Leninist and not even a Marxist in his basic ideology, to deal with this particular interlocutor.

Reggie was also an animating presence in the Campus Draft Opposition, a student-faculty organization that sponsored the Vietnam Commencement of May 17, 1968—thirty-six years to the day before he was run over by a truck and killed a few hundred yards from the spot—at which 773 draft-eligible students took an oath not to serve if drafted, supported by more than 300 faculty who stood that day on the steps of Sproul Hall in defiance of a ban the Regents had placed on the event.[7] Reggie was of course among them, and so was I, eligible, again, because of my title as Acting Instructor. That same semester, Reggie and I co-taught an undergraduate seminar on the history of conscription and resistance to it in modern European and American history. The course was "above load," taught voluntarily in addition to our regular teaching assignments, and met alternately at my apartment on Cedar Street and his house on El Dorado Street.

It was in co-teaching this seminar that I came to realize even more fully than before the success with which Reggie both combined and separated his professionalism as an academic and his politics as a citizen. These two parts of Reggie sat comfortably together in a single self, an integrated personality impressive for its capacity to maneuver adroitly in shifting contexts. In commenting on a student paper or leading a seminar discussion Reggie displayed the same style of reasoned, evidence-based argumentation that characterized his political discourse. But he knew that the warranted content of the subject matter it was his job to teach had its own integrity apart from how it might indirectly advance his own politics. He was strict with himself in keeping his teaching to what was accepted by the relevant community of professional scholars. He often made a point of praising the scholarly work of historians in his own field of Russian history whose politics were very different from his own.

This ability to be simultaneously political and professional while keeping each aspect in its own domain was a major reason, I believed in 1968 and believe even more confidently today, that Reggie won and retained year after year the respect and trust of so many faculty and students of quite different orientations and priorities. And the duration of Reggie's impact on the Berkeley campus demands special emphasis here, since my account focuses on the dramatic events of the 1960s that first defined him as a campus figure. The "state funeral" in The Glade would not have drawn so many hundreds, nor generated so many testimonials from persons of different generations, had Reggie been only a heroic relic of times long gone. The qualities of charisma and devotion to principle that Reggie displayed in Harmon Gymnasium in 1966 remained essential to him, and were seen in countless, more modest settings in later decades.

Never one to grandstand, and privately contemptuous of colleagues who played to the political galleries or used their classes as platforms for political proselytizing, Reggie taught and wrote as a historian, not as an ideologue. He understood the limits of scholarship's ability to change the world, and he also understood the damage political sectarianism could do to scholarship and teaching. Other Berkeley historians of his generation bore a similar witness, and, like Reggie, had a profound effect on me and many others of my generation. Yet it was Reggie's exemplification, in particular, of this profession-and-politics balance that was, to many of us, the most commanding.

At a time when all too many faculty depended on the approval of student radicals for self-assurance, Reggie was psychologically strong enough to go his own way, and to resist the enormous imperatives of the late 1960s to translate everything—including one's teaching, scholarship, social life, and intimate relationships—into political terms. If he was brave enough to risk the disapproval of colleagues for being "too radical," he was brave enough to risk the disapproval of student demonstrators for being "too conservative." This is not to say he was in the middle of the road. He knew there was more than one road, and he traveled each with intelligence, dignity, and wit.

To underscore Reggie's resistance to the wholesale politicization of life I want to recount a disturbing conversation I had in the spring of 1968 with a senior faculty member whom I will not name. It may seem a trivial incident, but in the context of worries I then had about the translation of every waking thought and deed into political terms, it shook me deeply. I still have total recall of it, to the point of remembering the no-longer-existing liquor store on Solano Avenue (Michael's) in which the conversation took place, and even the brand of scotch (King George IV) I was holding in my hand ready to purchase. Standing in the cashier's line next to me I noticed an older professor, the author of a book I was then reading with great admiration. I knew this eminent scholar slightly and understood that he was on the "other side." He was a vocal critic of the Faculty Peace Committee and the Campus Draft Opposition, two organizations in which he knew I was involved. But I was not thinking about politics that evening. I got his attention, and began to say something about his book, but he interrupted me and said very sternly, "Hollinger, don't you realize that when the revolution comes, liberals like you will be the first to be shot?" I was not sure what to say after that. Someone cleverer than I, and less shocked, might have made a good argument out of it. But confronted with the fact that he could see me only as a political being, I made a banal reference to how he and I disagreed about the Vietnam Commencement being planned by the CDO, and the two of us, having purchased our liquor, walked off in different directions on Solano. I knew my direction in life would always be different from his, partly as a result of the influence of an antithetical character in the drama of Berkeley in the '60s, Reginald Zelnik.

NOTES

1. This report was later published as a book; see Caleb Foote, Henry Mayer, et al., *The Culture of the University* (San Francisco: Jossey-Bass, 1968).
2. Martin Roysher, "Recollections of the FSM," in Robert Cohen and Reginald E. Zelnik, eds., *The Free Speech Movement: Reflections on Berkeley in the 1960s* (Berkeley and Los Angeles: University of California Press, 2002), p. 149.

3. Reginald Zelnik, "On the Side of the Angels: The Berkeley Faculty and the FSM," in Cohen and Zelnik, *The Free Speech Movement*, p. 291.

4. See the oral histories of Schorske and Stampp conducted by Ann Lage for the Bancroft Library: *Kenneth M. Stampp: Historian of Slavery, the Civil War, and Reconstruction, University of California, Berkeley, 1946-1983*, An Oral History Conducted by Ann Lage, Regional Oral History Office, Bancroft Library, 1998, also available at http://sunsite.berkeley.edu/uchistory/archives_exhibits/histories_interviews/oral_histories/; and *Carl E. Schorske: Professor of European Intellectual History, University of California, Berkeley, 1960-1969*, An Oral History Conducted by Ann Lage, Regional Oral History Office, Bancroft Library, 2000.

5. Leon Litwack, "Reginald Zelnik," *California Monthly* (September 2004), p. 53.

6. Peter Dale Scott, Franz Schurmann, and Reginald Zelnik, *The Politics of Escalation in Vietnam: A Citizens' White Papers* (Boston: Beacon Press, 1966). This book carried a preface by Arthur M. Schlesinger, Jr., and a postscript by Carl E. Schorske.

7. This event is described in Leon Wofsy, "When the FSM Disturbed Faculty Peace," in Cohen and Zelnik, *The Free Speech Movement*, p. 352.

APPENDIX 1

Reginald E. Zelnik's Doctoral Students and Their Major Publications*

Richard Donald Lewis, PhD 1971

"The Labor Movement in Russian Poland in the Revolution of 1905-1907." PhD dissertation

"Labor-Management Relations in Russian Poland," in *East European Quarterly*, Vol. 7, No. 4 (1973-74).
Revolution in the Countryside: Russian Poland, 1904-1907 (Pittsburgh: Carl Beck Papers, No. 506, 1986).
"Marxist Historiography and the History Profession in Poland, 1944-55," in John Morrison, ed., *Eastern Europe and the West* (New York: St. Martin's Press, 1992).
Multicultural Voices. (New York: McGraw Hill, 2000).

St. Cloud State University, *Professor of History*

Henry Reichman, PhD 1977

"Russian Railway Men and the Revolution of 1905." PhD dissertation

"Tsarist Labor Policy and the Railroads, 1885-1914," in *The Russian Review*, Vol. 42, No. 1 (1983).
Railwaymen and Revolution: Russia, 1905 (Berkeley and Los Angeles: University of California Press, 1987).
Censorship and Selection: Issues and Answers for Schools (Chicago: American Association of School Administrators / American Library Association, 1988).
"The 1905 Revolution on the Siberian Railroad," in *The Russian Review*, Vol. 47, No. 1 (1988). Japanese edition, 1993.
"On Kanatchikov's Bolshevism," in *Russian History/Histoire Russe*, Vol. 23, Nos. 1-4 (1996).

California State University, Hayward, *Professor of History*

Gerald Surh, PhD 1979

"Petersburg Workers in 1905: Strikes, Workplace Democracy, and the Revolution." PhD dissertation

"Petersburg's First Mass Labor Organization: The Assembly of Russian Workers and Father Gapon:" Parts I and II, in *The Russian Review*, Vol. 40, Nos. 3 and 4 (1981).

1905 in St. Petersburg: Labor, Society, and Revolution (Stanford, CA: Stanford University Press, 1989).

Special Issue of *Russian History/Histoire Russe*, Vol. 23, Nos. 1-4 (1996). Festschrift for Reginald E. Zelnik. Co-editor with Robert Weinberg.

"The Petersburg Workers' Organization and the Politics of 'Economism', 1900-1903," in *Workers and Intelligentsia in Late Imperial Russia: Realities, Representations, Reflections*, ed. Reginald E. Zelnik (Berkeley: International and Area Studies, University of California at Berkeley, 1999), pp. 116-144.

"Ekaterinoslav City in 1905: Workers, Jews, and Violence," in *International Labor and Working-Class History*, Vol. 64 (Fall 2003).

North Carolina State University, *Associate Professor of History*

Victoria Anne Palmer King, PhD 1982

"The Emergence of the St. Petersburg Industrial Community, 1870-1905: The Origins and Early Years of the Petersburg Society of Manufacturers." PhD dissertation

Deborah Lee Pearl, PhD 1984

"Revolutionaries and Workers: A Study of Revolutionary Propaganda among Russian Workers, 1880-1892." PhD dissertation

"Educating Workers for Revolution: Populist Propaganda in St. Petersburg," in *Russian History*, Vol. 15, Nos. 2-4 (1988).

"Political Economy for Workers: A. N. Bakh's *Tsar-Golod*," in *Slavic Review*, Vol. 50, No. 4 (1991).

"Tsar and Religion in Russian Revolutionary Propaganda," in *Russian History*, Vol. 20, Nos. 1-4 (1993).

"From Worker to Revolutionary: The Making of Worker *Narodovol'tsy*," in *Russian History*, Vol. 23, Nos. 1-4 (1996).

Tales of Revolution: Workers and Propaganda Skazki in the Late Nineteenth Century (Pittsburgh, PA: University of Pittsburgh, Center for Russian and East European Studies, University Center for International Studies, 1998).

Cleveland State University, *Associate Professor of History*

Isabel Tirado, PhD 1985

"Youth in Revolution: The Petrograd Komsomol Organization, 1917-1920." PhD dissertation

Young Guard!: The Communist Youth League, Petrograd, 1917-1920 (New York: Greenwood Press, 1988).

The Village Voice: Women's Views of Themselves and Their World in Russian Chastushki of the 1920s. The Carl Beck Papers, No. 1008. (Pittsburgh, PA: University of Pittsburgh, Center for Russian and East European Studies, 1993).

"The Komsomol and Peasant Women: Political Mobilization in the Village," in *Russian History*, Vol. 23, Nos. 1-4 (1996).

"The Komsomol and the Bright Socialist Future," in Corinna Kuhr-Korolev, Stefan Plaggenborg and Monica Wellmann, eds., *Sowjetjugend 1917-1941: Generation zwischen Revolution und Resignation* (Essen: Klartext, 2001).

"Peasants into Soviets: Reconstructing Komsomol Identity in the Russian Countryside of the 1920s," in *Acta Slavica Iaponica*, Vol. XVIII (2001).

William Patterson University, *Dean, College of Social Sciences and Humanities*

Lynn Mally, PhD 1985

"Blueprint for a New Culture: A Social History of the Proletkul't, 1917-1922." PhD dissertation

Culture of the Future: The Proletkult Movement in Revolutionary Russia (Berkeley and Los Angeles: University of California Press, 1990).

"The Rise and Fall of the Soviet Youth Theater TRAM," in *Slavic Review*, Vol. 51, No. 3 (1992).

"Performing the New Woman: The Komsomolka as Actress and Image in Soviet Youth Theater," in *Journal of Social History*, Vol. 30, No. 1 (1996).

"Shock Workers on the Cultural Front: Agitprop Brigades during the First Five-Year Plan," in *Russian History*, Vol. 23, Nos. 1-4 (1996).

Revolutionary Acts: Amateur Theater and the Soviet State, 1917-1938 (Ithaca, NY: Cornell University Press, 2000).

University of California, Irvine, *Professor of History*

Robert Etter Weinberg, PhD 1985

"Worker's Organizations and Politics in the Revolution of 1905 in Odessa." PhD dissertation

The Revolution of 1905 in Odessa: Blood on the Steps (Bloomington, IN: Indiana University Press, 1993).

Special Issue of *Russian History/Histoire Russe*, Vol. 23, Nos. 1-4 (1996). Festschrift for Reginald E. Zelnik. Co-editor with Gerald Surh.

Stalin's Forgotten Zion: Birobidzhan and the Making of a Soviet Jewish Homeland (Berkeley and Los Angeles: University of California Press, 1998). Published in French as *Le Birobidjan, 1928-1996* (Paris: Edition Autrement, 2000), and in German as *Birobidshan: Stalin's vergessenes Zion* (Frankfurt: Verlag Neue Kritik, 2003).

Special Issue of *Russian Studies in History*, Vol. 43, Nos. 1 and 2, 2004. Selected recent articles by Russian historians on Russian-Jewish history. Also wrote introduction.

"The Russian Right Responds to Revolution: Visual Depictions of Jews in the Black Hundred Press in Post-1905 Russia," in Ezra Mendelsohn et al., *Jews and the Russian Revolution of 1905: Essays in Honor of Jonathan Frankel* (Jerusalem: Hebrew University Press/Oxford University Press, forthcoming).

Swarthmore College, *Professor of History*

Laurie Bernstein, PhD 1987

"Sonia's Daughters: Prostitution and Society in Russia." PhD dissertation

Sonia's Daughters: Prostitutes and Their Regulation in Imperial Russia (Berkeley and Los Angeles: University of California Press, 1995).

"The Evolution of Soviet Adoption Law," in *Journal of Family History*, Vol. 22, No. 2 (1997).

"Communist Custodial Contests: Adoption Rulings in the USSR after the Second World War," in *Journal of Social History*, Vol. 34, No. 4 (2001).

"Fostering the Next Generation of Socialists: *Patronirovanie* in the Fledgling Soviet State," in *Journal of Family History*, Vol. 26, No. 1 (2001).

Editor, *My Life in Stalinist Russia: An American Woman Looks Back*, by Mary M. Leder (Bloomington, IN: Indiana University Press, 2001). Also co-author of introductory essay.

Rutgers University, Camden, *Associate Professor of History and Director of Women's Studies*

Mark David Steinberg, PhD 1987

"Consciousness and Conflict in a Russian Industry: The Printers of St. Petersburg and Moscow, 1855-1905." PhD dissertation

Moral Communities: The Culture of Class Relations in the Russian Printing Industry, 1867-1907 (Berkeley and Los Angeles: University of California Press, 1992).

Cultures in Flux: Lower Class Values, Practice and Resistance in Late Imperial Russia, co-edited and introduced with Stephen Frank (Princeton, NJ: Princeton University Press, 1994).

The Fall of the Romanovs: Political Dreams and Personal Struggles in a Time of Revolution, co-authored with Vladimir Khrustalëv (New Haven, CT: Yale University Press, 1995).

Proletarian Imagination: Self, Modernity, and the Sacred in Russia, 1910-1925 (Ithaca, NY: Cornell University Press, 2002).

Voices of Revolution, 1917 (New Haven, CT: Yale University Press, 2002).

University of Illinois at Urbana-Champaign, *Professor of History*

Stephen Kotkin, PhD 1988

"Magnetic Mountain: City Building and City Life in the Soviet Union in the 1930s, A Study of Magnitogorsk." PhD dissertation

Steeltown, USSR: Soviet Society in the Gorbachev Era (Berkeley and Los Angeles: University of California Press, 1991).

Magnetic Mountain: Stalinism as a Civilization (Berkeley and Los Angeles: University of California Press, 1995).

Armageddon Averted: The Soviet Collapse, 1970-2000 (New York: Oxford University Press, 2001).

Princeton University, *Professor of History*

Glennys Young, PhD 1989

"Rural Religion and Soviet Power, 1921-1932." PhD dissertation

"Bonch-Bruevich, Vladimir Dmitrievich." in *Modern Encyclopedia of Religions in Russia and the Soviet Union*, Vol. 4. (Gulf Breeze, FL: Academic International Press, 1991).

"Trading Icons: Clergy, Laity, and Rural Cooperatives, 1921-28," in *Canadian-American Slavic Studies*, Vol. 26, Nos. 1-3 (1992).

" 'Into Church Matters': Lay Identity, Rural Parish Life, and Popular
Politics in Late Imperial and Early Soviet Russia, 1864-1928,"
in *Russian History*, Vol. 23, Nos. 1-4 (1996).

*Power and the Sacred in Revolutionary Russia: Religious Activists in the
Village* (University Park, PA: Pennsylvania State University Press, 1997).

"Terror in *Pravda*, 1917-1939: All the News That Was Fit to Print,"
in Catherine Evtuhov and Stephen Kotkin, eds., *The Cultural
Gradient: The Transmission of Ideas in Europe, 1789-1991*
(Lanham, MD: Rowman & Littlefield, 2003).

University of Washington, Seattle, *Associate Professor of History and
International Studies*

David Wolff, PhD 1991

"To the Harbin Station: City Building in Russian Manchuria, 1898-
1914." PhD dissertation

Rediscovering Russia in Asia: Siberia and the Russian Far East, co-
authored with Stephen Kotkin (Armonk, NY: M.E. Sharpe, 1995).

To *the Harbin Station: The Liberal Alternative in Russian Manchuria,
1898-1914* (Stanford, CA: Stanford University Press, 1999).

*"One Finger's Worth of Historical Events": New Russian and Chinese
Evidence on the Sino-Soviet Alliance and Split, 1948-1959.*
(Washington, DC: Woodrow Wilson International Center for
Scholars, Cold War International History Project, 2000).

"Interkit: Soviet Sinology and the Sino-Soviet Rift," in *Russian History*,
Vol. 30, No. 4 (2003).

Cold War International History Project, Woodrow Wilson Center for
International Scholars, *Senior Research Scholar*

E. Anthony Swift, PhD 1992

"Theater for the People: The Politics of Popular Culture in Urban Russia,
1861-1917." PhD dissertation

"Fighting the Germs of Disorder: The Censorship of Russian Popular
Theater, 1888-1917," in *Russian History/Histoire Russe*, Vol. 18,
No. 1 (1991).

"Kul'turnoe stroitel'stvo ili kul'turnaia razrukha? (Nekotorye aspekty
teatral'noi zhizni Petrograda i Moskvy v 1917 g.)," in *Anatomiia
revoliutsii. 1917 god v Rossii: massy, partii, vlast'*, ed. V. Iu.
Cherniaev. (St. Petersburg: Glagol, 1994).

"Workers' Theater and 'Proletarian Culture' in Pre-revolutionary Russia, 1905-1917," in *Russian History/Histoire Russe*, Vol. 23, Nos. 1-4 (1996).

"The Soviet World of Tomorrow at the New York World's Fair, 1939," in *The Russian Review*, Vol. 57, No. 3 (1998).

Popular Theater and Society in Tsarist Russia (Berkeley and Los Angeles: University of California Press, 2002).

University of Essex, *Lecturer in History*

Julie Kay Mueller, PhD 1992

"A New Kind of Newspaper: The Origins and Development of a Soviet Institution, 1921-1928." PhD dissertation

"Soviet Journalists: Cadres or Professionals?," in *Russian History/ Histoire Russe*, Vol. 23, Nos. 1-4 (1996).

"Staffing Newspapers and Training Journalists in Early Soviet Russia," in *Journal of Social History*, Vol. 31, No. 4 (1998).

China, Maine, *Independent Scholar*

Lisa Ann Kirschenbaum, PhD 1993

"Raising Young Russia: The Family, the State, and the Preschool Child, 1917-1931." PhD dissertation

"Gender, Memory, and National Myths: Ol'ga Berggol'ts and the Siege of Leningrad," in *Nationalities Papers*, Vol. 28, No. 3 (2000).

" 'Our City, Our Hearths, Our Families': Local Loyalties and Private Life in Soviet World War II Propaganda," in *Slavic Review*, Vol. 59, No. 4 (2000).

Small Comrades: Revolutionizing Childhood in Soviet Russia, 1917-1932 (New York: RoutledgeFalmer, 2000).

"Scripting Revolution: Regicide in Russia," in *Left History*, Vol. 7, No. 2 (2001).

West Chester University, *Associate Professor of History*

Susan Katharine Morrissey, PhD 1993

"More 'Stories about the New People': Student Radicalism, Higher Education, and Social Identity in Russia, 1899-1921." PhD dissertation

Heralds of Revolution: Russian Students and the Mythologies of Radicalism (New York: Oxford University Press, 1998).

"From Radicalism to Patriotism: Petersburg Students between Two Revolutions, 1905-1917," in *Revolutionary Russia*, Vol. 13, No. 2 (2000).

"Patriarchy on Trial: Suicide, Discipline, and Governance in Imperial Russia," in *The Journal of Modern History*, Vol. 75, No. 1 (2003).

"In the Name of Freedom: Autocracy, Serfdom, and Suicide in Russia," in *Slavonic and East European Review*, Vol. 82, No. 2 (2004).

"Drinking to Death: Vodka, Suicide, and Religious Burial in Russia," in *Past and Present*, Vol. 186 (2005).

School of Slavonic and East European Studies at University College London, *Senior Lecturer in History*

Girish Narayan Bhat, PhD 1995

"Trial by Jury in the Reign of Alexander the II: A Study in the Legal Culture of Late Imperial Russia, 1864-1881." PhD dissertation

"The Moralization of Guilt in Late Imperial Russian Trial by Jury: The Early Reform Era," in *Law and History Review*, Vol. 15, No. 1 (1997).

"The Particulars of Guilt: Final Questions for the Jury Under the 1864 Judicial Reform." in *Canadian-American Slavic Studies*, Vol. 38, No. 3 (2004).

State University of New York College at Cortland, *Associate Professor of History*

Robert Paul Geraci, PhD 1995

"Window on the East: Ethnography, Orthodoxy, and Russian Nationality in Kazan, 1870-1914." PhD dissertation

"Ethnic Minorities, Anthropology, and Russian National Identity on Trial: The Multan Case, 1892-96," in *The Russian Review*, Vol. 59, No. 4 (2000).

Of Religion and Empire: Missions, Conversion, and Tolerance in Tsarist Russia, co-edited with Michael Khordarkovsky (Ithaca, NY: Cornell University Press, 2001).

Window on the East: National and Imperial Identities in Late Tsarist Russia (Ithaca, NY: Cornell University Press, 2001).

University of Virginia, *Associate Professor of History*

Benjamin Nathans, PhD 1995

"Beyond the Pale: The Jewish Encounter with Russia, 1840-1900."
PhD dissertation

"Habermas's 'Public Sphere' in the Era of the French Revolution," in
French Historical Studies, Vol. 16, No. 3 (1990).

*A Research Guide to Materials on the History of Russian Jewry (19th and
Early 20th Centuries), in Selected Archives of the Former Soviet Union*
[in Russian] (Moscow: Blagovest, 1994) [Vol. 4, Russian Archive Series].

"On Russian-Jewish Historiography," in Thomas Sanders, ed.,
*Historiography of Imperial Russia: The Profession and Writing of
History in a Multi-National State* (Armonk, NY: M.E. Sharpe, 1999).

"Die Vereinigten Staaten—das gelobte Land der Osteuropaforschung?"
in *Osteuropa*, Vol. 49, No. 8 (1999).

Beyond the Pale: The Jewish Encounter with Late Imperial Russia
(Berkeley and Los Angeles: University of California Press, 2002).

University of Pennsylvania, *Associate Professor of History*

D'Ann Rose Penner, PhD 1996

"Pride, Power, and Pitchforks: A Study of Farmer-Party Interaction on
the Don, 1920-1928." PhD dissertation

The Agrarian 'Strike' of 1932-33 (Washington, DC: Woodrow Wilson
Center for Scholars, Kennan Institute for Advanced Russian Studies, 1998).

"Stalin and the 'Ital'ianka' of 1932-1933 in the Don Region," in
Cahiers du Monde russe, Vol. 39, Nos. 1-2 (1998).

"Archival Ports of Entrance into the Worlds of Don Farmers in the
1920s," in *Cahiers du Monde russe*, Vol. 40, Nos. 1-2 (1999).

The Art of Research in Provincial Russia (Toronto, ON: University of
Toronto, Centre for Russian and East European Studies, 2002).

*Golod: 1932-1933 gody v sovetskoi derevne (na materialakh
Povolzh'ia, Dona i Kubani)*, co-athored with Viktor Kondrashin
(Samara, Russia: Samara University Press, 2002).

University of Memphis, *Associate Professor of History*

K. Page Herrlinger, PhD 1996

"Class, Piety, and Politics: Workers, Orthodoxy, and the Problem of
Religious Identity in Russia, 1881-1914." PhD dissertation

"Orthodoxy and the Experience of Factory Life in St. Petersburg, 1881
-1905," in Michael Melancon and Alice Pate, eds., *New Labor*

History: Worker Identity and Experience in Russia, 1840-1918
(Bloomington, IN: Slavica Publishers, 2002).

"Raising Lazarus: Orthodoxy and the Factory *Narod* in St. Petersburg, 1905-1914," in *Jahrbücher für Geschichte Osteuropas*, Vol. 52, No. 3 (2004).

Bowdoin College, *Assistant Professor of History*

William Arthur McKee, PhD 1997

"Taming the Green Serpent: Alcoholism, Autocracy, and Russian Society, 1881-1914." PhD dissertation

"Sobering Up the Soul of the People: The Politics of Popular Temperance in Late Imperial Russia," in *The Russian Review*, Vol. 58, No. 2 (1999).

"Sukhoi zakon v gody pervoi mirovoi voiny: prichiny, kontseptsiia i posledstviia vvedeniia sukhogo zakona v Rossii: 1914-1917 gg.," in N. N. Smirnov, et al., eds., *Rossiia i Pervaia mirovaia voina* (St. Petersburg: D. Bulanin, 1999).

CityBridge Foundation, *Program Officer*

John Wyatt Randolph, PhD 1997

"The Bakunins: Family, Nobility, and Social Thought in Imperial Russia, 1780-1840." PhD dissertation

"The Old Mansion: Revisiting the History of the Russian Country Estate," in *Kritika: Explorations in Russian and Eurasian History*, Vol. 1, No. 4 (2000).

" 'That Historical Family': The Bakunin Archive and the Intimate Theater of History in Imperial Russia, 1780-1925," in *The Russian Review*, Vol. 63, No. 4 (2004).

University of Illinois, Urbana-Champaign, *Assistant Professor of History*

Jeffrey John Rossman, PhD 1997

"Worker Resistance under Stalin: Class and Gender in the Textile Mills of the Ivanovo Industrial Region, 1928-1932." PhD dissertation

"Weaver of Rebellion and Poet of Resistance: Kapiton Klepikov (1880 -1933) and Shop-Floor Opposition to Bolshevik Rule," in *Jahrbücher für Geschichte Osteuropas*, Vol. 44, No. 3 (1996).

"The Teikovo Cotton Workers' Strike of April 1932: Class, Gender, and Identity Politics in Stalin's Russia," in *The Russian Review*, Vol. 56, No. 1 (1997).

"A Workers' Strike in Stalin's Russia: The Vichuga Uprising of April 1932," in Lynne Viola, ed., *Contending with Stalinism: Soviet Power and Popular Resistance in the 1930s* (Ithaca, NY: Cornell University Press, 2002).

Worker Resistance under Stalin: Class and Revolution on the Shop Floor (Cambridge, MA: Harvard University Press, forthcoming 2005).

University of Virginia, *Assistant Professor of History*

Ilya Vinkovetsky, PhD 2002

"Native Americans and the Russian Empire, 1804-1867." PhD dissertation

"Classical Eurasianism and Its Legacy," in *Canadian-American Slavic Studies*, Vol. 34, No. 2 (2000).

"Circumnavigation, Empire, Modernity, Race: The Impact of Round-the-World Voyages on Russia's Imperial Consciousness," in *Ab Imperio*, Vols. 1-2 (2001).

"The Russian-American Company as a Colonial Contractor for the Russian Empire," in Alexei Miller and Alfred J. Rieber, eds., *Imperial Rule* (Budapest and New York: Central European University Press, 2004).

Simon Fraser University, *Assistant Professor of History*

Victoria Sophia Frede, PhD 2002

"The Rise of Unbelief Among Educated Russians in the Late Imperial Period." PhD dissertation

"Istoriia kollektivnogo razocharovaniia: druzhba, nravstvennost' i religioznost' v druzheskom krugu A. I. Gertsena - N. P. Ogareva 1830-1840-kh gg.," in *Novoe literaturnoe obozrenie*, Vol. 49 (2001).

East Carolina University, *Assistant Professor of History*

Lisa Kay Walker, PhD 2003

"Public Health, Hygiene, and the Rise of Preventative Medicine in Late Imperial Russia, 1874-1912." PhD dissertation

United States Department of Health and Human Services, *Contractor for the Biotechnology Engagement Program*

* This list is limited to those students whose dissertations Reggie formally chaired and does not include the many students whom he mentored, advised, and on whose dissertation committees he served.

Copies of the dissertations listed here can be found in the Doe Library at the University of California at Berkeley. They can also be purchased from University Microfilms.

CURRICULUM VITAE: REGINALD E. ZELNIK

March 2004

BORN
May 8, 1936, New York, NY

HOME ADDRESS
1975 El Dorado, Berkeley, CA 94707-2441
Tel: Home: (510) 524-3083 or 525-2219
         Work: (510) 642-2457
Fax: (510) 643-5323
E-Mail: zelnik@socrates.berkeley.edu

EDUCATION
BA (magna cum laude), Princeton University, 1956
MA and PhD, Stanford University, 1961/1966

MILITARY SERVICE
US Navy, active duty 1957-59

PROFESSIONAL EMPLOYMENT
Indiana University, Bloomington
     Lecturer, 1963-64
University of California, Berkeley
     Acting Assistant Professor & Assistant Professor, 1964-70
     Associate Professor, 1970-76
     Professor, 1976 to present
     Chair, Center for Slavic and East European Studies, 1977-80
     Vice-Chair, History
          for Graduate Studies, 1986-87, 2003-05
          for Personnel, 1991-93
     Acting Chair, November-December 1992
     Department Chair, 1994-97

PROFESSIONAL SERVICE
Editorial boards, current
Journal of Social History, Kritika
Editorial boards, past
American Historical Review, Journal of Modern History, Slavic Review
Co-editor of series: "The Working Class in European History," University of Illinois Press, current
Board of Directors, National Council for Eurasian and East European Research, current
Advisory Council of the Department of History, Princeton University, current
SSRC/ACLS Joint Committee on Soviet Studies
Member, 1989-93
Chair (renamed: SSRC/ACLS Joint Committee on the Soviet Union and Its Successor States), 1993-95
AHA representative on Board of Directors of the American Association for the Advancement of Slavic Studies (AAASS), 1986-88
AHA and AAASS program committees: past member of each
Reviewer for university presses: University of California, Stanford, Princeton, Indiana, Northern Illinois, Pennsylvania State
Consultant, "Berkeley in the '60s" film project
Board of Directors, FSM Archive (nonprofit organization)

UNIVERSITY AND DEPARTMENTAL SERVICE (current only)
Chair of Executive Committee, Institute for Slavic, East European and Eurasian Studies
Member, International and Area Studies Committee Governing the Armenian Chair and Advisory Board, William Saroyan Endowment for Armenian Studies
Department Head Graduate Advisor, Placement Officer, Personnel Committee

COMMUNITY SERVICE (current only)
Member of Board of Directors, Mental Health Association of Alameda County

AWARDS/HONORS

Fulbright Fellow, 1956-57 (University of Vienna)

IUCTG grant, 1961-62 (Leningrad University)

Senior Fellow, Russian Institute, Columbia University, 1968-69

Guggenheim Fellow, 1971-72

ACLS Fellow, IREX Senior Exchange with Soviet Academy of
Sciences, 1972

Research Fellow, Historische Kommission zu Berlin, 1976

Ford Foundation Research award, Soviet and East European Studies,
1976-78 (co-recipient)

NEH awards
Translation grant, 1980-81; Conference grant, 1982;
Research Fellow, 1984

Bay Area Book Reviewers Association Translation Award, 1986

Fellow of the Center for the Advanced Study of the Behavioral
Sciences (Stanford), 1989-90

University of California President's Humanities Research Grant,
1989-90

Fellow of UC Berkeley's Townsend Humanities Center, 1990-91

Humanities Research Grant (UC Berkeley), 1993-94

IREX Special Projects Grant for conference in St. Petersburg,
June 1995: "Workers and the Intelligentsia"

American Historical Association's Nancy Lyman Roelker Mentorship
Award, 1996 (graduate mentoring)

Special Recognition Award for graduate teaching, presented at
History Commencement, 1996

Festschrift presented in honor of 60th birthday at ceremonial dinner,
18 May 1996

Humanities Research Grant (UC Berkeley), 1997-98

Distinguished Teaching Award (Social Science Division, UC
Berkeley), 1998

SELECTED PUBLICATIONS

Excludes book reviews, published conference commentaries, and
other brief communications; an asterisk (*) indicates a nonacademic
publication.

Books

Co-author (with Franz Schurmann and Peter Dale Scott)
The Politics of Escalation in Vietnam (Beacon, 1966;
Fawcett pbk, 1966).

Author

> *Labor and Society in Tsarist Russia: The Factory Workers of St. Petersburg, 1855-1870* (Stanford University Press, 1971).

Editor and translator

> *A Radical Worker in Tsarist Russia: The Autobiography of Semën Ivanovich Kanatchikov* (Stanford University Press, 1986).

Author

> *Law and Disorder on the Narova River: The Kreenholm Strike of 1872* (University of California Press, 1995).

Editor

> *Workers and the Intelligentsia in Late Imperial Russia: Realities, Representations, Reflections* (Berkeley, International and Area Studies, 1999).

Co-editor (with Robert Cohen)

> *The Free Speech Movement: Reflections on Berkeley in the 1960s* (University of California Press, 2002).

Articles and essays

> "The Sunday-School Movement in Russia, 1859-1862," *Journal of Modern History*, June 1965.

> "An Early Case of Labor Protest in St. Petersburg: The Aleksandrovsk Machine Works in 1860," *Slavic Review*, September 1965.

> * "Prodigal Fathers and Existential Sons: A Report from Berkeley," *Dissent*, May-June 1966.

> "The Peasant and the Factory," in *The Peasant in Nineteenth-Century Russia*, ed. Wayne Vucinich (Stanford, 1968).

> "Populists and Workers: The First Encounter Between Populist Students and Industrial Workers in St. Petersburg, 1871-74," *Soviet Studies*, October 1972.

> "Soviet Materials on Industrial Workers and the Labor Question," *European Labor and Working Class History*, November 1972.

> "Russian Workers and the Revolutionary Movement," *Journal of Social History*, Winter 1972-73.

> "Two and a Half Centuries of Labor History," *Slavic Review*, September 1974.

> "Russian Bebels: An Introduction to the Memoirs of Semën Kanatchikov and Matvei Fisher," Parts 1 and 2, *Russian Review*, July and October 1976.

> "Passivity and Protest in Germany and Russia: Barrington Moore's Conception of Working-Class Responses to Injustice," *Journal of Social History*, Spring 1982.

Annotated translation of selections from Semën Kanatchikov's
memoirs, published as Ch. 1 of *The Russian Worker: Life and
Labor in Tsarist Russia*, ed. V. E. Bonnell (University of
California Press, 1983).

"Wie Es Eigentlich Gegessen: Some Curious Thoughts on the Role
of Borsch in Russian History," in *For Want of a Horse: Choice
and Chance in History*, ed. John Merriman (Stephen Greene
Press, 1985).

"From Felons to Victims," *Representations*, No. 22, Spring 1988.

"Circumstance and Political Will," in *Party, State and Society in
the Russian Civil War*, ed. Diane Koenker et al. (Indiana
University Press, 1989).

" 'To the Unaccustomed Eye': Religion and Irreligion in the
Experience of St. Petersburg Workers in the 1870s," *Russian
History/Histoire Russe*, Vol. 16, Nos. 2-4, 1989. Reprinted
in *Christianity and the Eastern Slavs, II: Russian Culture in
Modern Times*, ed. R. Hughes and I. Paperno (University of
California Press, 1994).

*"On Schizophrenia, Reductionism, and Family Responsibility,"
Tikkun, January-February 1990. Partially reprinted as
"Blaming the Victims," *Utne Reader*, May/June 1990.

"Two Cheers for Gorbachev," *Tikkun*, November-December 1991.

"Before Class: The Fostering of a Worker Revolutionary,
Construction of His Memoir," *Russian History*, Vol. 20, 1993.

Nine entries in *Biographical Dictionary of European Labor Leaders*
(London, 1995).

"Not the Juice but the Juicer: On No Longer Existing Socialism and
Lemonade," *Contention*, Fall 1993. Reprinted in *Beyond Soviet
Studies*, ed. Daniel Orlovsky (Washington, DC, 1995).

"On the Eve: An Inquiry into the Life Histories and Self-Awareness
of Some Worker-Revolutionaries," in *Making Workers Soviet*,
ed. Lewis Siegelbaum and Ronald Suny (Ithaca, 1994).

"The Fate of a Russian Bebel: Semën I. Kanatchikov, 1905-40,"
Carl Beck Papers, No. 1105, 1995.

"International Colloquium on Workers and the Intelligentsia in
Russia in the Late Nineteenth and Early Twentieth Centuries,"
in *International Labor and Working-Class History*, Spring 1996
(co-author).

"Revolutionary Russia, 1890-1914," in *Russia: A History*, ed.
G. Freeze (Oxford, 1997).

"Rabochie i intelligentsiia v 1870-kh gg.," in *Rabochie i intelligentsiia*, ed. S. I. Potolov, et al. (St. Petersburg, 1997).

"Workers and Intelligentsia in the 1870s: The Politics of Sociability," English version of previous Russian article, in *Workers and the Intelligentsia in Late Imperial Russia: Realities, Representations, Reflections*, ed. and intro. by R. E. Zelnik (Berkeley, IAS, 1999).

"Introduction," Festschrift for Richard Stites; special issue of *Journal of Popular Culture*, Spring 1998.

"*Weber* into *Tkachi*: On a Russian Reading of Gerhart Hauptmann's Play *The Weavers*," in *Self and Story in Russian History*, ed. Laura Engelstein and Stephanie Sandler (Cornell University Press, 2000).

"Carl Schorske and Berkeley's Time of Troubles," *Chronicle of the University of California*, Spring 2002.

" 'On the Side of the Angels': The Berkeley Faculty and the FSM," in *The Free Speech Movement: Reflections on Berkeley in the 1960s*, ed. Robert Cohen and R. E. Zelnik (Berkeley, 2002).

"A Paradigm Lost? Response to Anna Krylova," *Slavic Review*, Vol. 62, No. 1 (Spring 2003).

"Worry about Workers: Concerns of the Russian Intelligentsia from the 1870s to *What Is to Be Done?*" in *Extending the Borders of Russian History: Essays in Honor of Alfred J. Rieber*, ed. Marsha Siefert (Central European University Press, 2003).

"Workers," and "Union of Struggle for the Emancipation of Labor"; entries in *Macmillan Encyclopedia of Russian History*, in press

"Anna Pankratova as Victim and Victimizer, 1920-1957: The Troubled Life of a Soviet Historian," forthcoming as a separate publication in the *Donald W. Treadgold Papers* series; title subject to change.

SELECTED RECENT (SINCE 1993) CONFERENCE PAPERS AND RELATED ACTIVITIES

Paper

"Workers and Intelligentsia: Representation and Self-Representation," at First Russian-American Summer Seminar, "Russian History and Culture in World Context," Smolensk, Russia, August 1993.

Paper

"Law and Disorder: Views from Estland and St. Petersburg," SSRC workshop on "Visions, Institutions, and Experiences of Imperial Russia," Washington, DC, September 1993 (member of conference coordinating committee).

Discussant
>   Center for the History of Freedom, Washington University, St. Louis,
>   1993; Conference on "The Ambiguities of Revolution."

Session Chair
>   25th AAASS National Convention, Honolulu, November 1993;
>   "Off Nevsky: Towards a Cultural Geography of St. Petersburg."

Session Chair
>   "The Archive in Russia," Berkeley Conference, "The Russian
>   Archive: Cultural History and Contemporary Practice," March 1994.

Conference Co-chair
>   "Workers and Intelligentsia," International colloquium on history of
>   the working class of Russia, second half of the 19th - beginning of
>   the 20th centuries, St. Petersburg, 12-16 June 1995.

Paper
>   "Workers and Intelligentsia in the 1870s," International colloquium
>   listed above, 12- June 1995.

Commentator
>   Panel on "Time and Money in Imperial Russia," 19th Annual
>   Berkeley-Stanford Slavic Studies Conference; "Time and Money in
>   Russian Culture," Berkeley, March 1995.

Paper
>   "The Historical Background to the Crisis in Russia," Post-Charter
>   Day UC Alumni Seminar, April 1995.

Paper
>   "Weber into *Tkachi*: A Reading," SSRC Conference on "Self and
>   Story," San Diego, CA, September 1996.

Panelist
>   28th AAASS National Convention, panel on "Categories of Social
>   Identity and Social Analysis in 19th- and 20th-Century Russia,"
>   Boston, November 1996.

Commentator
>   29th AAASS National Convention, panel on "Text and Context:
>   The Russian Workers' Movement, 1900-1917," Seattle,
>   November 1997.

Paper
>   "What was a 'Strike'?" Russian History Conference at UCLA,
>   April 1999.

Paper
>   "The Law in Late Imperial Russia," Stanford University, 24th
>   Annual Berkeley-Stanford Slavic Studies Conference, April 2000.

Roundtable participant

32nd National Convention of AAASS, "Workers and Society in Russian History," Denver, CO, 11 November 2000.

Commentator

Panel on "Memories, Generations, and Life Histories in the Making of Post-Communism," 25th Annual Berkeley-Stanford Slavic Conference, Berkeley, March 2001.

Panel chair

"Vietnamization of the Berkeley Campus," in "Taking Part: FSM and the Legacy of Social Protest," symposium sponsored by Bancroft Library and the University Library, Berkeley, 14 April 2001 (member of the conference's organizing committee).

Co-chair and convener

"All-California Conference on Russian History," UC Berkeley, 2 1-22 April 2001.

Commentator

Discussant for four papers at International Colloquium "Vlast' i nauka, nauka i vlast' / Scholars and Politics; Knowledge and Power, from the 1880s to early 1920s," St. Petersburg, 6-9 June 2001.

Paper

"The Idea of the Worker on the Russian Left," 27th Annual Berkeley-Stanford Slavic Studies Conference, "The Power of Ideas and Ideas of Power in Eastern Europe and Eurasia," Berkeley, March 2003.

Paper

"Ni bes ni angel: Anna Pankratova as Victim and Victimizer, 1920-1957: The Troubled Life of a Soviet Historian," March 2003, Stanford University, at "Shaping Memory, Shaping Identity in Russian History," workshop in honor of Prof. Terence Emmons.

Lectures, interviews and readings on The Free Speech Movement: Reflections on Berkeley in the 1960s (see listing of books above), at: Cody's, A Well Lit Place for Books; Bookmarks; KGO Radio; German TV ("ARD"'s KULTURWELTSPIEGEL); and Le Nouvel Observateur.

CURRENT AND FUTURE PROJECTS (in progress)

• Biography of the Soviet labor historian Anna Mikhailovna Pankratova, focusing on her troubled political and professional life from ca. 1920 to her death in 1957. This short book of ca. 100 pages will analyze several telling moments in Pankratova's career as the most powerful woman in the Soviet

Union's history profession. It is conceptualized as a study of what I call "constrained dissent," whereby a Communist scholar who was somehow simultaneously devoted both to the cause of the Party (*"partiinost'"*) and to serious historical scholarship managed to survive a series of near disasters in her (almost inseparable) private and public lives. Often "swimming underwater," as the saying went, Pankratova managed to survive exile, purges, the arrest of her husband, and expulsion from the Party, sometimes contributing to the victimization of others yet at times acting bravely to defend her friends, students, and colleagues from ruin. A leading voice for the liberalization of Soviet historiography in the early Khrushchev years, she died a sad death in 1957, abandoned by Khrushchev, her erstwhile protector, and the Party leadership. Her story is in many ways more interesting and revealing than those of the more well-known dissidents on the one hand and the full-fledged conformists on the other. My study, which does not purport to be the kind of definitive and exhaustive biography that the subject deserves, is based mainly on previously inaccessible archival materials and memoirs published in Russia since the fall of the Soviet régime in 1991, and to a lesser extent (for the 1950s) on microfilmed Soviet archives at the Hoover Institution. The writing is nearing completion.

• Chapter on the history of Russian workers and the pre-Revolutionary labor movement for the new *Cambridge History of Russia*, Volume 2: *1689-1917*, edited by Dominic Lieven (London School of Economics). Ca. 10,000 words, to be completed May 2004.

• The Meaning of Strikes, 1789-1917. A long-term project in comparative history, still at an early stage of research. In addition to the comparative dimension, the project entails exploration of the influence that the experience (and representations of that experience) in one society had on the evolution of ideas and practices in the other, with Russia seen as the main "follower" or recipient of influence in most but not all cases. The research focus includes the interaction between factory workers and the very different legal systems of Imperial Russia, Prussia/Germany, and 19th-century France, with special focus on those legal scholars, jurists, and political thinkers who wished to apply the rule of law to industrial relations by staking out positions on the right to strike. Although some archival research is involved, I am exploiting the existence of numerous journals, document collections, and other published sources, including a rich secondary literature, in order to do much of the work locally. My interests include the rights and wrongs of striking in the thought and representations of scholars, political figures, and nonacademic writers of fiction such as Gerhart Hauptmann, author of the play *Die Weber*, and Emile

Zola, whose *Germinal* (under various titles) and *Le Travail* were widely read in Russian translation, including abridged versions for the working people (*narod*). This will be part of a larger *Begriffsgeschichte* of the "strike" (and the deployment of that concept in actual strikes) in all its linguistic, social, and political transformations from the French Revolution, when strikes and guilds were denounced by revolutionaries in the name of freedom, to the Russian Revolutions of 1905 and 1917, when the strike became a quintessential symbol of revolutionary action. (I have not decided whether to extend the study from 1917 to 1921, an interesting period in which Bolshevik authorities, longtime advocates of the strike, had to find a new language with which to *denounce* those strikes that were seen as inimical to the new Soviet régime.) Although my ultimate aim is the completion of a book, that is a long way off, and I anticipate writing and publishing related articles well before a book has been drafted. I have already given an unpublished, very preliminary paper on the subject (at UCLA) and have published a related essay on Hauptmann's play, which is based on the great Silesian strike of 1844 and which had a significant influence on the Russian Left (see "Publications," above).